HER
PHOENIX
RISING

Hope this Collection
of stories stirs something
inside of you!

be.
luul. CC

HER PHOENIX RISING

A JOURNEY TO HEALTH AND HEALING THROUGH SELF-LOVE

CHRISTIN COLLINS

NEW DEGREE PRESS

HER PHOENIX RISING

A Journey To Health and Healing Through Self-Love

ISBN   978-1-63676-951-6   *Paperback*

978-1-63730-017-6   *Kindle Ebook*

978-1-63730-119-7   *Ebook*

You can change people's lives, including your own, through love and kindness.

DAVID COLLINS

Dedication

To my husband, David, who has supported all of my crazy since day one. You have taught me that all things are possible, and I am eternally grateful.

CONTENTS

———

AUTHOR'S NOTE   11

PART 1. **FOUNDATIONAL LESSONS**   **15**
MEGHAN'S INSPIRATION   17
PLANNED PARENTHOOD SAVED MY LIFE   21
30,000 FEET   31
ROUND ONE   35
DAVID COLLINS   41

PART 2. **A SHIFT IN PERSPECTIVE**   **49**
BENNETT'S DONUTS   51
UNEXPECTED HEALING   57
MY WAKE-UP CALL   65
WHOLE FOOD   71
UNCHARTED WATERS   75
SYSTEM DIRECTOR HEALTH & WELLNESS   87
THE WELLNESS WHEEL   91
IN THE STATE OF INFLAMMATION   95
GRAM   99

PART 3. THE INNER WORK **107**

THE DIVA 109

ROOT CAUSE 115

MANIFESTING MY REALITY 119

UNDER THE TUSCAN SUN 127

RECEIVING 139

INSPIRE AWAKENING 143

LIGHTHOUSE 149

PART 4. LETTING GO AND AWAKENING WITH PURPOSE **159**

SAYING YES TO THE UNIVERSE 161

UNATTACHED TO OUTCOME 169

MY STINT AS A POLITICIAN 177

LOBBY BAR 187

134 BITS OF INFORMATION 199

THE DAY I KNEW I HAD TO LEAVE HEALTH CARE 205

PART 5. RISING TO NEW BEGINNINGS **211**

EPILOGUE 213

ACKNOWLEDGMENTS 217

AUTHOR'S NOTE

———

Smack dab in the middle of my life, I found myself going through a modern-day mid-life crisis. Fifty years in hot pursuit of happiness, wealth, tropical vacations, fancy things, a loving marriage, and all the glitter and gold that we pursue during our time on this planet.

I had it all.

Have you ever been on vacation, but instead of being present and enjoying it, you were planning your next trip? Or three weeks after bringing home that upgraded car you thought would be the best thing ever, you found yourself starting to fantasize about the next car you'd get in three years once the lease on this one was up? How about that promotion at work or—better yet—a pay raise?

This was literally me. The minute I obtained that new purse or drank that very delicious and expensive bottle of wine, I was searching for what would be next. The more I seemed to consume, the hungrier I found myself to be.

This type of consumption isn't sustainable, and something deep inside of me finally got my attention. I honestly forget which disappointment had just occurred, or what thing I was trying to control that blew up in my face. However, one day right around my fiftieth birthday, I heard these incredibly clear questions bubble up from inside of me.

What's the purpose of all of this?

Why are we here?

Is this all there is?

Life can be insane. I felt like I was perpetually on a gerbil wheel, spinning round and round and round with no clear destination in sight, and certainly not leading to true meaning and satiation. This self-realization caused me to pause.

I mean really, truly pause.

I was excelling at work, incredibly involved in serving my community, and focused on being loving and generous. My family was equally amazing, my marriage was incredible, and my surroundings were plush. So what was missing? Why was I constantly searching for the next thing? And why was my health far from thriving? All of these questions opened the path to an incredible journey.

This book is my reflection of my journey and how it has led to more vibrant health and personal wellbeing. It documents my navigation toward true health, which required intense physical, mental, emotional, and spiritual collaboration.

These stories share how I've learned to sit with myself, and get really, really comfortable in my own skin.

To know, love, and forgive myself, and those who have hurt me.

To release judging others.

To sit in the present moment and let go of what I don't control.

To find my inner connectivity, voice, and wisdom.

I had to stop allowing distractions to prevent me from reconnecting with my inner knowing and let the rest magically unfold. On this journey, I've met many people who, like me, are searching. Sometimes, exactly what they're searching for is unclear. Or, perhaps, they are too distracted and busy to even notice they're trying everything and anything to fill a deeply rooted inner void.

Something has brought this book into your life, whether it was a friend who suggested it, a post you saw on social media, or a gift from the universe. Are you open to finding the root cause of your void, take a pause, sit with it, and heal? In order to find true health and happiness, we must each make an authentic connection to ourselves, which involves both self-love and introspection. I believe it's from this place of honesty and wholeness that we can become who we were created to be.

These stories are an act of healing. I share all of this without shame, sadness, or ego in hopes that when you absorb them, something inside of you stirs. My life's purpose is to achieve and inspire awakening. I'm on the discovery path to actualize this purpose, experience total wellbeing, stop filling my void with external stimuli, and become whole through self-love, care, and actualization. May this collection of stories inspire you as you begin or continue your journey.

be.
love.
CC

PART 1

FOUNDATIONAL LESSONS

MEGHAN'S INSPIRATION

———

LATE 2015

It was a warm, southwest Florida evening, and I sat on
my back lanai with my husband, David, and stepdaughter,
Meghan, taking in the damp air, the smell of the salty water-
way, and the sounds of nature settling in for the evening. The
rustling of the wind in the trees, soft splashing of the water
against the dock, and the whispering of crickets created a
symphony of calmness and serenity. The sun set behind us
as I exhaled with fullness and that pleasant, tired feeling
you get when you've put in another full day and can marvel
at your output.

David has been my biggest supporter since the day I met
him twenty years earlier on a blind date on which neither
of us wanted to go. His steady, calm, intuitive support laid
a foundation for me so that I could take risks for my own
personal growth. While he encouraged me, he also kept me
tethered to reality. Without David, I would've come out of
the gate too hot and intense and would have crashed and
burned quickly.

Another gift that David gave me was the opportunity to create a family with his two beautiful children. I met the kids when Brendan was seven and Meghan was five. Since then, I've soaked up the opportunity to be a part of their growth and upbringing. My journey as a stepmom has been one of my greatest joys, and this particular pleasant Florida night was one of those extra special moments that ripped my heart wide open and planted seeds that would affect me for decades to come.

Meghan was working toward her master's degree in clinical social work. Since meeting her fifteen years earlier, she had developed a knack for saying the most profoundly deep things in a quiet, concise manner; they were like atomic bombs of wisdom, coming out of her tiny body with big blue eyes. Throughout the years, these one-liners would occasionally arise, and I would stop dead in my tracks. That night, she said, "People are on their own journey, healing from early experiences, and finding their way."

Wait. . . what did she just say? How does she know that? I'm more than twenty-five years older than her, and I just figured that out last week!

What a blessing to share life with such an old soul. I had no doubt that our connection wasn't an accident. We were meant to walk this lifetime together, and I cherished the opportunity to be a Collins.

As David, Meghan, and I sat out back, we reflected on another hardship that I had navigated and learned from. It wasn't often that the three of us had time to sit together at home, delve deep into conversation, and celebrate the reflection. Fortunately, this was one of those very special evenings.

As we were concluding our deep dive into the wonder of the journey, Meghan looked at me with her immense kindness and compassion and said quietly, "It's amazing what you've been through throughout your life. And you not only survived but have grown through it all to become as successful as you are. No one knows this about you. Your life looks so easy and carefree from the outside. You would help inspire so many people if they had any idea what you've overcome. You should share your stories and write a book. It would inspire others. They'd know that if you could do it, they can, too."

Boom.

I felt like the whole planet had just shifted as I let her words sink in. Deep. I had a soft spot for helping others, so if there was anything I could do to support someone else's growth, I was *in*.

She was right. She was always right. My life did appear rather fun and easy from the outside. Don't get me wrong, sometimes it was. But I'd also been through a number of major life experiences that were incredibly difficult. Not one or two, but many. Yet, there I sat, stronger and more alive than ever, giving thanks for the opportunity to experience and grow from my wounds.

That was the moment that planted the seed for this book. "You should write a book. You should share your stories." I'd heard it before—including from David—but I hadn't been ready to open myself up to the idea. That humid Florida night, as we sat together on the back lanai, this book idea actually began to grow.

PLANNED PARENTHOOD SAVED MY LIFE

———

SUMMER 1990

It was a hot, glorious, sunshiny day at the Woodbridge Country Club. I was perched at the entry table by the pool, safe-guarding the towels and welcoming the occasional member to sign in. I'd wrapped up my undergrad experience at the University of Connecticut a few weeks earlier and was back home with my parents, taking a stab at adulting.

My dad was the pool director at the club and had offered me a job managing the towels and member sign in. It was 1990, and the New England economy was in shambles. Unemployment soared, so while putting my college degree to work and getting a teaching job was my goal, each position available received over two hundred applicants and staff reductions continued to rise. I felt very thankful to take this job basking in the sun by the poolside and dreamed of the day when I would be lounging as a member instead of as the hired help.

As the day moved toward lunchtime, I perused the club menu to decide what to order for lunch. This was usually the biggest decision of my day, so I took my time and gave it my full attention. Suddenly, I heard someone clearing their throat. Startled, I looked up from the menu to find a young man standing in front of me. I was surprised to see him, since the average member that I encountered was retirement age or older. This particular man looked to be around my same age or maybe just a few years older. It was refreshing to see someone my own age. I smiled, apologized for being distracted by my lunch choice, and asked him to sign in.

Instead of signing in, he extended his hand toward me, and simply introduced himself.

Polite. I liked it.

"Hi, I'm Christin. I'm the pool director's daughter. I'm working here for the summer."

He smiled slowly and replied,

"I heard."

Have you ever had an experience where you knew something was about to change? You knew that a particular moment in time was going to have major significance, yet you had no idea how, when, where, or why? This was one of those rare moments.

Instead of heading to the pool, he pulled up a chair and joined me at the check in table. He stayed for hours. We ordered lunch and ate together leisurely, just chatting. He was charming and made me feel like I was the only thing that mattered on the planet. I let it happen, even though I knew it was crazy. Others let it happen too; members and staff watched as this beginning unfolded, and no one intervened or said a word. Time blew by and stood still at the same time, and before I knew it, the pool was closing, and it was time to go home.

"Let me take you to dinner."

Are you crazy? We just talked for like five hours. Shouldn't we slow down? You're a member and I'm the pool attendant. You're rich. I'm not. There are so many reasons to end this here, now. You're dangerous. I have no idea what you see in me, and I'm not comfortable putting myself out there just to end up getting hurt.

But instead, I heard myself respond something different.

"Sure."

A few short hours later, a very large Mercedes Benz rolled up into my parent's driveway, and off we went for dinner. My world was spinning, and I knew I was heading for the edge of the cliff. While this relationship logically made no sense to me, every inch of my body knew this man was going to be a big thing in my life. I knew that we were going to go for a ride, and that it was going to be dangerous, out of control, and fun as hell.

I hadn't been sexually active for over a year. In college, we were blessed with amazing health care, so birth control was available and appreciated. I had no health insurance as a recent college grad pool attendant, but I knew that I needed to get a move on and figure out quickly how to get myself back on the pill. It took a few weeks for the pill to be up and running in my body, and I hoped that I could wait that long before the inevitable happened. Time was of the essence!

He and I were inseparable after our chance encounter, so a few days later I called my high school friend and asked her if she had any spare birth control pills.

"I don't," she shared. "But there is this place in New Haven that gives away free birth control pills. Here's the phone number, give them a call."

And give them a call I did. Immediately. They provided their physical address, and set up an appointment for the following day.

The next day I found myself driving into the bowels of New Haven, frankly a bit concerned for my safety. I parked, scurried into the building, and let the front office person know who I was, and that I was here for the free birth control. She escorted me to a patient room, instructed me to undressed from the waist down, and wait for the attending clinician. My nerves were a bit rattled, but I followed instruction, and waited for the nurse to arrive.

The nurse was pleasant as can be and shared that she was going to perform a routine exam before authorizing birth control.

Whatever. Do what you need to do, as long as you give me the pill so I can move on with my life and new relationship.

The exam seemed routine enough, lasting only a few minutes or so. She finished, instructed me to get dressed, and let me know that she would be back in a few minutes.

Perfect. She was going to go get my pills, and I would be back on the road in a few moments.

She re-entered the room as promised, without pills in hand. Instead, she sat down in a vacant chair, and looked at me squarely.

"During your exam, I felt an abnormality on your right ovary. I am not sure what it is, but I'm concerned about it. I have scheduled you to come back on Wednesday at 12:15 p.m. so you can see a doctor from Yale-New Haven Hospital. He volunteers one hour a week for us during his lunch hour, and sees four patients. I want you to be one of them."

Seriously! Are you crazy? Listen, I'm sure you're a nice person, but this is a free clinic, and you probably don't really even know what you're doing. Can't you just give me my birth control pills and let me get on with my life?

"Okay, thank you. I will be back on Wednesday and appreciate your help."

As I left this weird, kind of scary place, I called a few additional friends to see if they might have some birth control pills I could use so that I wouldn't have to go back there. No one had any extra. Who knew this would be such a pain? Time was ticking, and I was very aware that things would be moving forward with pool guy soon. I felt frustrated by my bad luck and how I had hit a dead-end road.

On Wednesday at 12:15 p.m., I was back in the clinic being examined by the doctor. He was a stoic, kind man, with whom I felt immediately comfortable. He examined me and confirmed that he felt the same abnormality that the nurse had felt in my original examination.

"Christin, you will need to come to the hospital tomorrow, where I will perform exploratory surgery. I don't know what this is, but we need to open you up and take a look. Is there someone who can drive you to Yale tomorrow for this procedure?"

What? What the heck is happening?

"Well, sure, if that's what I need to do. I can ask my Mom to bring me. I'm scheduled to teach an aerobics class tomorrow night. . . do I need to get a sub?"

The doctor smiled.

"Yes, go ahead and get a sub. I'll see you and your mom at 7:00 a.m. tomorrow. Here's the address and phone number if you need anything."

The following morning, my mom and I drove back into New Haven and entered the surgical waiting area at Yale. The receptionist asked me to fill out lots of paperwork and to create a living will. When they came to get me, I said goodbye to my Mom and told her that I would see her in a few hours.

Fourteen hours later, I woke up in recovery. I was disoriented, freezing cold, and my abdomen hurt a lot. I was pleasantly greeted by a nurse who asked me if I was cold. I told her that I was literally freezing, and could not seem to get warmed up. She piled more blankets on me, explaining that I was in the recovery area, and would be brought up to my room shortly.

A few hours later, I found myself waking up in a hospital room that I shared with three other patients. I was warmer now, but my stomach still ached and I was scared and disoriented. My parents weren't there, nor were there any clinicians, so I hit a call button by the bed to see if I could connect with anyone with answers.

A nurse answered the call and said, "Oh good, you're awake."

"I am. Where are my parents? And now that the surgery is over, can I take my first birth control pill to get that started?"

She replied, "Your parents went downstairs to get something to eat. I'll get the doctor and your parents so we can discuss your birth control."

Weird, but whatever. I hoped my parents would bring me something to eat since I hadn't eaten a darn thing all day.

The surgical resident who assisted with my procedure came into the room, and I smiled at her. She was learning her craft from the fine doctor, and it was inspiring to see this young woman about my same age rock out a medical career. She pulled up a chair by my bed, and began to share the story of my procedure privately with me before my parents returned.

"Well, it's a very good thing you went to Planned Parenthood in search of birth control. You were in surgery today for eleven hours. When we opened you up, we discovered a tumor on your right ovary the size of a grapefruit. It's astounding that you couldn't feel it. We biopsied this ovary, your left one, and your lymph nodes. You had ovarian cancer. Fortunately, it was contained in your ovaries and hadn't spread yet. You're incredibly lucky, but we did have to remove both of your ovaries. You still have a uterus, but your ovaries couldn't be saved."

Groggy from the meds and the eleven hours on the operating table, I tried to let this information sink in. The doctor told me I needed exploratory surgery. The word cancer never came up. I don't know a ton about the reproductive system, but I was pretty sure that my ovaries were fundamental to produce children. Without them. . .

"Thank you, Doctor. I have a question for you. Without ovaries, am I able to have children?"

"We felt your ovaries were too far gone to harvest and save any eggs from. But you still have your uterus. There will be ways for you to still carry a zygote, but you'll have to use an egg donor and inseminate."

A silence fell over the hospital room. I laid still and tried to absorb this information. I never was one of those girls who dreamed of their kids' names and played mommy with her dolls, yet I always assumed I'd have kids, a white picket fence, a husband, a dog, and drive carpool. What would it be like to not be able to have a child the traditional way? Who would want to marry me with this challenge? How would I go about getting an egg donor and what if my child wanted to find their "real" mom? So many questions swirled through my mind. I was scared, sad, confused, and overwhelmed.

"Ok, thank you for explaining. Why did I get cancer? What did I do wrong?"

"Oh Christin, if only I knew, I'd be a billionaire! No one knows why people get cancer."

With that, she smiled a slow, sad smile. She said goodbye and went off to help another patient.

My parents returned, incredibly thankful to see me awake and alive, and hugged me for what seemed like hours. The country club guy never stepped foot in the hospital during the nine days I was in there, confirming my intuition that this relationship would lead nowhere except to heartbreak. Yet, I was forever grateful for our fateful crossing. If I hadn't met him, if my girlfriend had an extra pack of birth control, if the doctor didn't volunteer an hour a week at Planned Parenthood, if Yale didn't take charity care. . . if, if, if, if. Why was I still here? Why did this series of events happen that ended up saving my life? What were the odds? God had blessed me with this second chance at living, so he must have something in store for me. Gifts and blessings show up in unexpected ways.

Without the health clinic which provided free care to my middle class, uninsured self, my outcome would have been very different. Without the caring staff and volunteers passionately providing council and services to tens of thousands of patients each year, how many others' lives might have played out differently as well.

Thank you, Planned Parenthood, for saving my life.

30,000 FEET

SUMMER 1999

Click, click, click.

I listened to the purposeful sound of my high heels briskly walking down the jet bridge as I headed toward my first flight of the day. As a flight attendant for American Airlines, I boarded the aircraft and stowed my luggage, well rested and ready to see what the day would offer up. I loved everything about my job, from its adventurous nature to all of the new people, places, hurdles, and joys I experienced. There was nothing mundane about traveling the world and seeing all the different walks of life.

I poked my head into the cockpit and introduced myself to the two strangers who now officially held my life in their hands. Rarely would I see the same face twice. I chose to fly purser, a role kind of like the chief flight attendant, since it put me in charge of the cabin. It was very important to me to set a tone of professionalism, approachability, unity, and kindness. I led by example in hopes that the crew and our passengers would have the best day possible.

My fellow flight attendants boarded the airplane, exchanging pleasantries and introduced themselves.

"Good morning!" my new colleague said. "I'm Diego. It's great to meet you. I just commuted in from Chicago."

"It's great to meet you, too," I replied. "Christin." I introduced myself, shaking his hand. His smile was warm and inviting, and I experienced gratitude to share this journey with him.

"Great, I'll go check the supplies in the back," Diego said, making his way toward the back of the plane. "When we get to Mexico City, I know of a great place to eat, if you and any of the others want to grab dinner."

This was one of my favorite parts of being a flight attendant. Strangers became instant colleagues. Walls didn't stand a chance. In order to do an exceptional job and enjoy the experience, it was best to open up very quickly and leave no room for judgement. By inviting fellow crew members into your world and experiences with open arms and love, we explored new destinations, meals, and cultures in one shared community. Diego was a new friend for a single moment in time. I was grateful.

The rest of the crew arrived with similar openness. I encouraged each of them to let me know if they needed anything, and expressed that I was happy to support them in any way.

The gate agent arrived at the boarding door, asked if we needed anything, and if it was ok to begin the boarding process. I said, "It's a go!" It was time to welcome the passengers on board. I stood at the front door, doing my best to personally greet each passenger as they entered.

"Hi there, welcome aboard! Do you know what seat you have? Please let me know if I can help you in any way."

I wanted the passengers to feel welcomed and to let each individual know that I saw them. It was an honor and a privilege to be part of every traveler's journey to their destination. All different walks of life took a flight, with each person having a different reason to be traveling on any given day. I pondered the why behind today's flight and appreciated how there were untold stories that I would probably never hear.

I've long had a knack for connecting with people very quickly. Upon reflection, I realize it was my days as a flight attendant that taught me how to do this. Think about it: 150 or so perfect strangers get into a metal tube with wings on it. We take off into the sky like a bird, soaring high above the clouds, breathing shared air. The faces are all different, and the experiences even more diverse.

For thirteen years, I met all kinds of people working as a flight attendant. I hugged strangers as they travelled to bury a loved one, a sudden loss from which they may never recover. I smiled at honeymooners giddy with excitement as they start their life together. I watched divorcees devastated by the destruction of their family life. I met people traveling for medical treatment, those heading to meet a new grandchild, business folks who carried the weight of the world on their shoulders, and single moms who faced the challenge of juggling their kids who never seemed to stop crying. To create a safe and pleasant experience, I needed to find commonality as quickly as possible.

To take flight, we set aside assumptions and biases and found unity to move us toward our shared destination. As in life, we often do not have the opportunity to truly know someone and to hear about their experiences that make them the unique person that they are. Being a flight attendant taught me how to embrace the diversity of us all as well as our differences of opinions without actually uncovering the background and history that we each bring to any given moment.

I am honored when I learn people's stories, but I also marvel at the mystery of those who are silent. As I performed the safety demonstration, and looked out at the sea of faces ready to take flight, there was one thing in common. There was a destination ahead and a purpose in their journey. They wanted to experience a life moment, to find answers. I couldn't possibly understand how they felt or what was going on inside their heads.

Whether it is a joyful celebration, or a traumatic heartbreak, we each have a purpose for our journey, and we each want to be seen, heard, and understood.

ROUND ONE

——

SUMMER 1999

I always knew I would never get a divorce. After living through the years of turmoil and heartache that defined the ending of my parents' marriage, I swore on my life I would never, ever get a divorce. I was smart and self-sufficient and would be able to select the right partner to walk my first and only marriage with. I was in no rush. I would wait for the right one to come along no matter how long the wait was.

At twenty-five, I met him. As I was licking battle wounds from recent relationship devastation, there he was on the dance floor. The music was pounding. The lights low and strobing. It was a Sunday night in a New Haven, Connecticut, night club. We had actually gone to high school together, though he was two years younger than me. While in high school, he'd played basketball and I was a cheerleader. I clearly remembered him because I found it ironic that he played basketball even though he was so short. Not only was he extremely short, but his best friend was incredibly tall. Those two were inseparable, and today I can still picture them walking down the hall at school together, a 2:1 ratio. I always liked his energy and his smile, and I was tickled pink that we were reconnecting now that we had both grown into our adult selves.

He asked me to marry him four years later. I was floored, as we had never discussed marriage. I was out of my head thrilled, as I opened my Christmas present that snowy Christmas Eve, and saw this over-the-top *fabulous* diamond ring. Holy wow! He was the right one; he was easy going, fun, driven, hard-working, successful, and I adored his family. I had found my haven. My identity. My safe harbor. My best friend.

Unfortunately, I bet you can guess how this story goes.

Eight months after our *very* expensive, public wedding, we were settling into bed on a Friday night. He had barely spoken a word to me all week. This was very unusual behavior, and I was sad and scared. In the dark, I whispered to him:

"Goodnight. I miss you."

I heard a long, deep exhale.

"Well, I guess I should say something to you," he replied sadly.

My heart suddenly began to pound loudly in my chest.

"Sure. If you're ready to, that would be great."

In a low, even tone, I heard him say, "I don't love you. I don't think I ever loved you. And I don't want to be married to you."

I laid in bed, paralyzed. *Please tell me this is just a very, very bad dream. There is no way this is at all possible.* I had just turned thirty. I waited so long to make sure I was with the right person. I didn't ask *him* to marry *me*. We didn't rush into anything. How could my life's greatest fear be coming true?

I heard myself say to him in a calm, surreal voice that couldn't possibly be my own, "I don't think this is about me. I don't think you know or like yourself. You can't love me if you don't know and like you."

The entire week he'd been acting so weird. On Monday, he had started a new job with a large company, where his look-alike father was the CEO. There, he had found his confidence. His swag. His high rolling, I-am-awesome self. Unfortunately, he found it because he was the son of the CEO of his new company, not because he'd finally discovered the beautiful light that was inside of him all along. I didn't understand this at the time. As I think back on this pivotal conversation, it was ironic that my response to him was ultimately spot on. However, I was right not because I was speaking from a place of expertise or deep insight, but because I, too, didn't know and love myself. At the time, we both thought we were whole and the right partners to build a lifetime together. It's amazing that I intuitively knew his conflict stemmed from not knowing himself, but it took me another few decades to thoroughly understand this about *my*self.

I fought for this marriage for almost two years. I'd said, "In sickness and in health, 'til death do us part," and I meant it. We would work through this. I believed in us.

We would attend family gatherings and confuse everyone in the room. "Are they together? Are they splitting up?" One day it would look like we could turn the corner and move forward united, but weeks of not connecting would follow. It was an incredibly confusing emotional roller coaster of uncertainty, hope, and sadness.

I went to therapy. Occasionally, he would join me. Therapy was not foreign to me; I'd spent quality time in therapy before, working my way through debilitating childhood experiences that no one should have to endure. I welcomed therapy as a tool to deeply explore life, relationship dynamics, and myself. I did my best to hold myself responsible for a part of this unexpected turn in our marriage.

While we were separated, I began to realize how much of my self-esteem and identity had become tied up in being his wife, taking on his last name, and marrying into his well-to-do family. I had confidence while wearing his ring. I had enjoyed the warmth of his loving family, the thrill of their lifestyle, and the ease of walking into a room with him. I had seen myself through the lens of being his wife, and suddenly, I was out in the world again by myself. The ring was stored somewhere. The country club was gone. The conversations I had at work on the airplane were uncomfortable and awkward, as I no longer knew how to be myself outside of my marriage.

One day, we decided to go for a long walk together around the beautiful neighborhood in which we had created a home. As we walked, the conversation that unfolded was tired, yet we were more honest and open than perhaps we had ever been.

We kicked the leaves with our feet as we strolled along, and I heard him say:

"People don't change."

I let that settle in and listened to the crunching of fallen leaves as we continued to walk along. I pondered how two people—two married people who waited four years to get married—could see things so differently.

"I don't see it that way. I think people change all the time. Do you think I'm the same person I was when you met me? Or the same as I was the day you married me? I'm ever evolving, learning, and growing from each experience that life tosses my way. I think it's the total opposite. People constantly change."

That was the day I knew we were not going to make it. There were so many conversations we hadn't had and so many that we didn't even know we *should* have had. We both had so much yet to learn, mostly about ourselves. Finally, we ended up divorced. I had lived out my biggest fear: I was a thirty-two-year-old divorcee, and I had no idea how to be me outside of being with him.

DAVID COLLINS

SEPTEMBER 1999

It was all set. I was moving back into New York City full time. The divorce had punctured my heart and soul. New York, with all its hustle and bustle, energized me. As a young flight attendant, I had enjoyed a shared midtown apartment with five girlfriends before retreating into the suburbs. I appreciated the rainbow of cultures and experiences all collected on this concrete peninsula. The city was the place I needed to retreat back in to reinvent myself again. As a thirty-two-year-old divorcee, who, by the way, could not naturally birth children, my life was not unfolding the way I thought it would. Hopefully, time in my favorite city would help.

As I prepared to leave the suburban Connecticut shoreline, a quick trip to visit my college roommate down in Florida was in order. Dana and I had been jetting down to her family condo in Naples since we were sophomores at the University of Connecticut. We loved to escape the unwelcoming cold of the Northeast. We both cherished the beaches, golf courses, shopping, and lifestyle that southwest Florida had to offer.

We soaked in the sun, drank our fair share of umbrella cocktails, and went bar crawling with the golf pros. This world was so different from our lives up north—so free and easy. I dreamt of the day I could own my vacation home in paradise.

Dana had moved to Naples the year prior, and I was excited to fly down to spend a much-needed weekend with her. I wanted to detach from my divorce, work, and life in general. This next chapter was destined for me to be alone, spending time licking my wounds. Being among the palm trees, miles of sandy beaches, and outdoor eateries would do the trick. When I arrived for my visit, Dana greeted me with one of her infamous surprises.

"Great news. I've set up three blind dates for you. Two are tonight."

Classic Dana. No rest for the weary. *Shake it off, move on, let's do this.* A mixture of amusement and distain washed over me.

"D, you're the sweetest. I truly appreciate you trying to help me out, but I have to be honest. I can't stand men. I have no desire to meet anyone right now. I just want to be alone."

Years of friendship had proven that Dana does not take "no" for an answer. Once this fun-loving, charismatic, go-getter sets her mind, she's unstoppable. So, a few hours later, seven of us stood in her kitchen sipping cocktails, waiting for my first blind date to arrive.

Earlier in the week, my first mystery blind date had helped his high school friend purchase a new home. As a successful mortgage banker, David Collins attended the closing with his client to ensure they addressed all the final details and things went smoothly. The realtor for this transaction happened to be Dana's mom. She was also a very successful professional who showed up to this closing in support as well.

With all parties seated at the closing table, Dana's mom asked David, pointedly,

"Who are you?"

"I'm David, the lender on this transaction. Nice to meet you."

"Hmm. Are you married?"

Taken aback, David paused for a moment, unsure how to answer, then decided to engage with her.

"I'm not married. Recently divorced, actually."

He hoped that would be enough to stop the inquiry. Rapid fire questions kept coming.

"Have any kids?"

With this one, David blushed. *Where was this lady going? How inappropriate was it to be asking me such personal questions at a closing table!*

"I do. I have a seven-year-old son and a five-year-old daughter."

"Perfect," Dana's mom replied. "My daughter's college room-mate is flying into town in a few days. You need to meet her."

The buyer laughed out loud, and attention turned back to the business at hand. Yet, Dana's mom had planted the seed, and the conspiracy to have David and Christin meet was set in motion.

Time was ticking away, and David had not arrived. Dana was not amused. As one of her guests was the high school friend and home buyer from said real estate transaction, he volunteered to call David to see what was holding him up. After many attempts, David answered his phone.

"I told you yesterday, I'm not coming. I have my kids and it's a Sunday night. I'm not even interested in dating right now. Thank you, but no thank you."

Ironically, David's friend was as stubborn and persistent as Dana. Begrudgingly, David finally agreed. His dad came by to cover the kids, and he began this thirty-minute drive south to meet up with us.

When David walked into Dana's condo, I was put out. For starters, I was embarrassed to be set up on a blind date and perfectly capable of meeting my own men in my own time, thank you very much. Second, it was apparent that David was not interested in meeting me, either. How incredibly uncom-fortable for both of us. Third, he immediately reminded me of home in Connecticut—of everything I was trying to leave. He was devilishly handsome with lush black hair and pierc-ing blue eyes. He had a strong, athletic build, a wide smile with perfect white teeth, and an air of confidence that came from a mixture of hard work, adventure, and lived experiences. He, too, was from New England, yet he chose Florida for his home. He was real and immediately familiar. I knew he was dangerous because he could potentially worm his way inside of my heart.

We barely said hello to one another and spent the next hour on opposite sides of the room. The eight of us made small talk, and decided to head to the beach to watch the sunset. I was relieved; fresh air would do me some good.

As we set out to depart, Dana and I were the last two to get outside. Her husband was behind the wheel of their car, with passengers in the back. She glided over to the passenger seat, and slid in next to him. Without looking back, they drove off.

I stood in the driveway, facing the remaining car. David sat in the driver's seat with his high school friend and wife in the back. One spot remained for me: his passenger seat. I let out a long, deep exhale and proceeded to get into his car. I hoped this ride would go quickly. I settled in and did my best to engage in conversation.

I asked David questions to which I already knew the answers. He got divorced a few months ago, had two kids and two cats, worked as a banker, grew up in Cape Cod, and played hockey at Assumption College. What I did not ask about was the pain and suffering that his heart must have been going through. Like me, we were both devastated about our divorces. This first blind date was too soon to be vulnerable, though. We were both just trying to survive our forced meeting.

Yet, as the night unfolded on the beach, we both started to lower our guards. We took in the warm fall Florida air and the glorious gulf coast sunset, and I began to relax.

"Sure, I'll have another drink. Thank you."

"Yes, I do love it down here."

"I love being a flight attendant and taking in the world."

"Naples holds a special place in my heart."

"I'd love to live here one day."

"The Florida lifestyle really speaks to me."

"New York City can be tiring."

"I'm not sure what the future holds."

A few hours later, the eight of us left the warmth of the sand and headed out to dinner. As we approached the cars, this time I did not hesitate to climb into David's passenger seat. I also naturally sat next to him at dinner. I asked him what he was ordering, so I could adjust my selection accordingly. When our food arrived, I helped myself to his dish, then scooped up a big spoonful of mine and fed it to him. I didn't even notice the other three couples staring at us.

David almost immediately fit like my favorite pair of jeans and snuggly sweater. He was perfect. Easy. Natural. Familiar.

I never met the second nor the third blind date. David was my destiny.

This destiny was not a streamlined fairy tale, however. We experienced many twists, turns, ups, and downs. Both of our hearts had been broken, and it took years for us both to heal and trust again. David had custody of his two beautiful children 50 percent of the time, but they were his priority 100 percent of the time. It was one of the things that attracted me most to him; his love for his children was all encompassing. I respected him so much for that. We endured many adjustments, sacrifices, and discomforts and took years to unfold our relationship respectfully for them.

Ultimately, I did forego life back in New York City, instead choosing Naples as my home. I left flying so I could be home more, as it devastated me to miss any of the kids' activities. After four years of dating, I was blessed to become David's wife and stepmom to Brendan and Meghan. Being a part of raising another couple's children was challenging and uncomfortable at times, but it was also the most rewarding experience of my life. It taught me to contemplate my motives and decisions before moving forward and taking action. It taught me unconditional love and blessed me with the honesty of childlike wonder. David's love was strong and true, and I never took it for granted. Becoming a part of the Collins family has blessed me with decades of growth, challenge, joy, and deep, deep love.

PART 2

A SHIFT IN PERSPECTIVE

BENNETT'S DONUTS

APRIL 2012

Have you ever met a complete stranger who single-handedly took your life in a completely different direction than you had ever imagined? Whether the crossing was a split second in time or a decade long unfolding, that person makes you wonder, *"What would my life have been like if we never met?"* Scott Kashman was that person for me—a complete stranger who turned into the most impactful partner in crime. We shared a fateful chance meeting that ultimately influenced and inspired a chapter that I definitely didn't see coming.

It was spring 2012. For the previous three years, I had been working for a large public health care system as a fundraiser for their foundation. My boss at the foundation was a woman of few words. She exuded power, strength, and a no-bull-shit approach. She had a reputation for making people cry. I was excited to work for her because she got things done. I didn't meet with her often, which was a blessing. It freed me to raise tens of millions of dollars to build our Children's Hospital using the style and tenacity that I saw fit.

Her hands-off approach worked well, as I was definitely a self-starting, non-traditional fundraiser.

One seemingly random day, my boss abruptly came into my office and asked if I would do her a favor. I had to admit, any time my boss walked into a room, even I got nervous. This particular occasion, I was *definitely* nervous. Having no idea what she wanted or potentially what I had done wrong, I held my breath and waited with anticipation.

"Would you please meet with the guy who is running Cape Coral Hospital? He's driving me crazy. He's been pestering me for a year wanting some help raising money for his campus. I keep telling him that we are already all-hands-on-deck building the Children's Hospital and cannot offer up any staff to fundraise for his campus. He just won't let up! Would you please connect with him so he feels heard?"

I was beyond excited to receive this request from my boss and was ready to squash this man's relentless pestering to alleviate her undue stress. This favor would certainly be a feather in my cap and would take almost no time or energy at all.

"Absolutely. It would be my pleasure. I'll take care of it right away." Within moments, I reached out to the perpetrator's assistant, and made arrangements to meet with Mr. Scott Kashman at a local coffee shop.

I woke up bright and early to meet this intrusive hospital executive. As I drove downtown, the sun was just coming up. I took in the royal palm trees that lined the street and appreciated how the sunrise glistened upon them. Life was good. I was blessed. And I was on a mission to quietly and succinctly exterminate the dreams of a man who was pestering my boss.

I arrived at Bennett's Donuts a few minutes ahead of schedule, ready to settle myself into a seat and prepare for the meeting. That was one of my tactics. Arrive early, scope out the scene, set the stage, and prepare for engagement. As I walked through the front door, the alluring smell of fresh baked donuts and exquisite coffee took my breath away. Yet, the smell wasn't the only thing that surprised me; Scott Kashman was already there, sitting at the corner table, which was already set up with coffee, oatmeal, and his VP of Nursing.

This scenario caught me off guard. For starters, I was early. He was *earlier*. This, I was not used to. Second, it was April in southwest Florida, which meant it was very, very hot out. This compact, wiry gentleman was buttoned up from head to toe in his dark colored, formfitting suit, starched white shirt, perfectly poised tie, shined shoes, and not a hair out of place. He definitely dressed the part for his executive role, and was laser focused to close his deal. Impressive. I was used to being the one in charge, but today I was face-to-face with a man on a mission.

As I worked to regain my composure and settle in, we exchanged pleasantries and introductions with one another.

"Well, thank you for the full-service breakfast upon arrival, Mr. Kashman. I appreciate you making sure I don't miss a meal."

Scott smirked and replied. "Who doesn't appreciate a healthy start to their morning and the delicious aroma of excellent coffee!"

Scott served as the executive running Cape Coral Hospital, the red-headed stepchild of the health care system. He was approachable, easy to talk to, and incredibly witty. I pondered how this intense, maverick New Yorker was ever selected to run this particular campus. Inside, I couldn't help but giggle. The people from The Cape must hate this guy. He definitely didn't fit in around these parts. As I contemplated why on God's green Earth he had taken this job, Scott launched into his vision for the hospital.

"I want to build an Optimal Healing Environment, creating a rallying point for our employees and community to get excited about. In partnership with the city, I want to host a space where people can come to be well and heal."

Please note, this was health care in 2012. Virtually no one was talking about "healing spaces" or health in general. Health care was a robust model of repairing illness and disease after its onset, using symptoms to diagnose and pharmacology and surgery to attempt to repair. While Scott's innovative idea was exciting for me to hear, it was not in alignment with the health care system's vision, nor health care in general. Plus, our foundation was busy raising funds for the Children's Hospital. As previously shared with him, we didn't have extra staff on hand to embrace this pie in the sky idea.

Still, I listened with amusement and a bit of curiosity. Scott's energy was through the roof. He had sparkling blue eyes that clearly showcased he was up to something without giving away enough to fully understand exactly what it was. I had always been a sucker for this. Often, I would also have a deep-seated intention, which would prove to be too disruptive for others to embrace or understand. The longer I sat and smirked, the more animated he became. It was clear he wholeheartedly believed in his idea, and was hell bent on manifesting it.

In hindsight, I'm honestly not sure how much time passed. It felt like a nano second, but at the same time, I swear he didn't take a single breathe for forty-five minutes. And suddenly, out of nowhere, he stopped. I felt like all of the oxygen had instantly been taken out of the room. He leaned in, and looked me straight in the eyes. I was caught off guard, yet I sat in the stillness of the moment, wondering what was about to happen.

"So, will you help me?"

Help him? Help him what? What was this guy talking about? What did he want me to do? What did he want anyone to do?

I had no concept of what he was asking. What I did know was that he was clearly very excited about his vision and that he was looking for someone who could help him advance his cause.

Without thinking, I heard myself speak.

"Yes."

Three little letters. One little word. *Yes. But what had I just said yes to? And why?*

I was sent in to listen and dissuade, to put to rest this over-zealous executive who clearly didn't understand that we were raising $100 million to support building a Children's Hospital. Instead, bubbling up from somewhere deep inside of me, I came up with "Yes." I knew this wasn't a strong career move on my part, and I was at a loss for how I would explain things when I got back to the office.

Ironically, I didn't care. From a place of knowing and heartfelt surrender, I had said yes. I felt free, light, and downright excited. Simultaneously, I had zero clarity on who, what, when, where, or how, but I did have a surreal feeling that this was going to be a very big yes. I wanted to help him. I *had* to help him. He was creating something much, much bigger than himself—something that I didn't yet understand, which excited the heck out of me.

I had met someone who would teach me incredible lessons about things I had yet to see. Sometimes in life, we're presented with opportunities and crossings that steer us in a direction we didn't see coming. When we're in touch with our instincts and intuition and present in the moment, we can find the courage to say *yes* to the universe and to ourselves. These life curveballs are incredible blessings when we surrender and embrace our inner knowing.

I knew that morning, over a cold bowl of oatmeal and half a cup of coffee, that my life was about to change, forever.

UNEXPECTED HEALING

———

MAY 2014

Awareness that some injuries and illnesses could not be explained or addressed by modern medicine was not an overnight realization for me.

My first exposure to this was, ironically, at a charity function. I stopped by an event at a local spa supporting one of my favorite non-profits. They were offering haircuts, nail services, and a few other things which I didn't need. They were also offering "readings." I was unsure what a reading was, but it wouldn't mess up my hair or nails, so I purchased it to be a supportive attendee of the event.

I entered one of the service rooms where a woman sat at a small card table with a deck of cards. *This is going to be fun*, I thought. I had never done anything like this. What a great adventure.

As I settled in, she asked me to shuffle the cards and divide them up a few different ways. We made small talk, and I smiled with amusement. I couldn't imagine what this woman could possibly offer me. I internally swore to keep a straight face and not react to any information she comes up with. There was absolutely no way I was going to feed into this.

We were about five minutes into my reading when she abruptly stopped. She looks up from the cards and addressed me with concern.

"How long have you had leaky gut?"

I'm taken aback. What is she talking about? I had heard the term once or twice before, as I had become concerned about stomach issues that had started showing up for me most afternoons. It was not a sudden awareness, but a slow origin that began in childhood. Over the past year or so, things had escalated to a daily bloat, discomfort, and, at times, emergent bowel issues. The medical community had immediately dismissed the term "leaky gut," however. There was no such thing as a leaky gut. Sitting there in a spa service room with a stranger and a deck of cards, she asked me about my digestive system. Weird.

Determined not to influence this experience, I simply replied, "I'm unsure what you're talking about."

Actually, that was the truth. I didn't know what she was talking about.

"Wow," she continued. "You must be in so much pain. You need to address this right away. You should go to an acupuncturist as soon as possible."

A lightbulb went off. *Now I get it! She must be an acupuncturist, or maybe her boyfriend is. She's trying to sell me services.*

Strategically, I responded, "Thanks for sharing. I don't have an acupuncturist. Do you have one you recommend?"

This would flush out the sales pitch, showing her for the fraud that she was.

"I'm sorry. I don't. But you need to find one quickly. You're in really bad shape and are doing irreversible damage to your body." She then turned her attention back to the deck of cards and switched subjects. I'm relieved to move on.

About five minutes later, she again paused and locked eyes with me.

"He has an accent."

Who has an accent? I wait, unsure what she was talking about or who *he* was. She continued.

"He's handsome. And tall. I think he's from Australia. His accent sounds Australian. You need to see him. He can help you."

Oh, we're back to acupuncture. I guess her boyfriend is tall and handsome and has an accent. Now we're getting to the sales pitch.

"Got it. I need to see this particular acupuncturist. By chance do you have his contact information?" *What a scam.*

"I don't. I don't know who he is. But he has an accent. And is handsome. You need to see him as soon as possible."

Thankfully, this reading wrapped up a few minutes later. I left with a mixture of amusement and frustration. How invasive of this woman to manipulate me and scare me with this leaky gut diagnosis? This type of thing should be outlawed.

The very next day, I was at the hospital plugging away in my office. It was still morning. For the past several months, I would experience severe discomfort and bloating after lunch-time. That day, it began closer to 10:00 a.m. My stomach was ahead of schedule. There was no clear reason as to why it had begun earlier than usual. There was actually no rhyme or reason to understand why it was happening at all. I couldn't concentrate on my work. My stomach was cramping and gurgling, causing increasing discomfort. After a dozen or so embarrassing trips to the shared public bathroom, I began to evaluate what I might be able to do to remove myself from this whole situation.

I stared at my computer screen, and found myself pulling up Google.

I searched, "Acupuncturist. Fort Myers." I clicked "Enter."

Suddenly, staring back at me was a handsome man. Angular. Lean. Direct, blue eyes. *That's hilarious. Of course a hot guy would be the first thing I see when I google acupuncturist. Can't make this stuff up.*

I decide to go ahead and call his office. What could I lose? I had to try something to get this stomach thing under control.

A very pleasant woman answered the phone and offered to set me up with an appointment. Dr. Murdock had an opening in three days. *Three days? I'm not sure how I'm going to get through the next three days.*

As if hearing my thoughts through the phone, the receptionist spoke up again.

"Oh, wait. He actually had a cancellation tomorrow morning, but it's in our Fort Myers office. I'm not sure if you'd want to drive all the way over there."

Apparently the number I had called was to his main office, located in the town north of Fort Myers.

"I actually live and work in Fort Myers. Can you tell me where he sees patients over here?"

His Fort Myers office was two miles from my home.

I booked the appointment.

I continued to navigate the remainder of the day by not consuming any food, and remaining seated as much as possible. It was a very uncomfortable experience.

The following day, I proceeded to my acupuncture appointment. A sign on the door that said "Take a seat, someone will be with you shortly!" greeted me. As I sat in the makeshift waiting area, I marveled at how I had lived two miles from this office space for over a decade but had never noticed it. I felt safe close to home yet unnerved by the unknown.

The door swiftly swung open, and out stepped a very tall, regal, and strikingly handsome man. I smiled with amusement, funny how things unfold sometimes. I stood up and extended my hand, ready to introduce myself to this stranger. Before I could say anything, he began.

"Hi. Great to meet you, Christin. I read the report from my receptionist at the main office. This is your first time receiving acupuncture, correct?"

I found myself at a loss for words, and actually sat back down in the chair I had just risen from. It wasn't Australian. It was close, but not Australian; it was British. He was totally from London. I had flown London for years as a flight attendant. I could pick out that accent anywhere. He was tall, handsome, and had an accent, just like that tarot card reader had said.

I worked to regain my composure, aware that I must appear to be scared to death of acupuncture.

"Thank you. Nice to meet you. You're correct, I've never had acupuncture before." I stopped speaking before I said something stupid.

"What brings you in today?"

Seriously, what should I tell him? *A few days ago, I went to a charity event at a day spa and got a tarot card reading. The reader said I had leaky gut and that a tall, handsome Aussie could help me.* I was seriously losing it.

"My stomach gets bloated and hurts. Someone mentioned that acupuncture might be able to help, so here I am."

And with that, my first office visit began. We discussed all sorts of things that can influence gut health. They were things I'd never discussed before—my microbiome, the bacteria in my gut, my chakras, the flow of energy in my body, and blockage. It was a foreign language to me, but I was so tired of being in pain that I was open to anything. As I listened, it kind of made sense. I decided to be open to the information and the experience. Needles in my body definitely freaked me out, but being exhausted and constantly having to find a bathroom upset me more.

I left the office visit, unaware that this was the first of many, many alternative healing modalities that I would explore. It was the start of approaching my health differently. It forged the focus on healing and releasing, all because of a tarot card reader at a charity event and an acupuncturist with a British accent. The journey would unfold as mysteriously as it began.

MY WAKE-UP CALL

NOVEMBER 2014

I jolted straight up in bed, suddenly wide awake from a dead sleep. The room was pitch black and the air bone-chilling cold, which made no sense because I lived in southwest Florida where it was almost always hot. The pain in the left side of my chest felt like something was knifing its way through my ribs from the inside, desperate to get out.

Where am I?

Am I having a heart attack?

*I need some help **now.***

Panic began to envelop me like a heavy, dark cocoon. I realized I was out of town in a hotel room, hence the unfamiliar surroundings and ice-cold air. David slept peacefully by my side, looking like a young child without a care in the world. I didn't want to wake him, yet the pain near my heart was escalating. Thoughts of being wheeled into a strange hospital emergency room frightened me.

Should I wake him and beg him to get me to an ER?

Time would be of the essence.

We needed to move fast before it was too late.

Torn with what to do, I tried to take a deep, exaggerated breath.

Breathe.

Take a moment, calm down.

Breathe.

Willing myself to lay back down, I zeroed in on taking deep breaths and worked to calm myself down. The pain in my chest was real and pounding away. I was confused, scared, and overwhelmed by the conflicting self-talk that was rampant inside of my head.

As I held eerily still, I worked to compartmentalize the rapid-fire thoughts and gain clarity on the situation. I was in health care after all. Surely I could figure this out if I remained calm and still.

David and I were in Nashville attending the Country Music Awards. We were having an absolute blast, embracing all that Nashville nightlife had to offer. The awards show led to bar hopping, boot scoot boogying, and a late-night date with a large pizza when we returned to the hotel. We laughed happily as we devoured the pizza in bed, the aroma of cheese overtaking my senses as I marveled at how blessed our lives were.

This following morning, we had an early flight back home. As mentioned, this very severe, sharp pain in my chest abruptly woke me up.

After spending what seemed like eternity talking to myself, I decided to gently wake David. It was almost time to head out to the airport anyway. As he came about, I shared with him the condition of my chest. Concern was written all over his face. He asked:

"What would you like to do? Should I call an ambulance?"

"Absolutely not. I'm sure it'll go away. Let's head over to the airport. This'll probably work itself out."

We proceeded to the airport, and I continued hoping the chest pain would dissipate as the day unfolded.

It did not. It stayed constant and severe. Our concern escalated. After boarding the plane, we texted our friend and colleague Dr. Brian Taschner, a cardiologist who promoted lifestyle medicine. I never actually saw him as a patient, as I had never needed a cardiologist. This time, I reached out as a potential patient and shared with him what was going on. He advised that I immediately go to an emergency room. I thought that was extreme, just a doctor being over-protective.

"Brian, we've already boarded the plane and are about to take off. If the pain is still there when we land, I'll head to the hospital to have things looked at. Thank you, we'll keep you posted."

When we landed back in Florida, the chest pain was bad. I was having trouble breathing, and the pain in my chest was excruciating. I looked at David, apologized, and asked him to take me to the emergency room.

Twenty minutes later, David whisked me into our hospital. I immediately underwent a series of tests. The emergency room doctor was young, proficient, and straight to the point. I felt a sense of relief that I was safe and that I would soon better understand what the heck was going on with me.

In less than an hour, the doctor was standing at my bedside, chart in hand. David and I listened eagerly, ready to take on whatever he was about to share.

"All of your tests look great. There's nothing wrong with you."

I found that confusing; I had a huge pain in my chest, was having difficulty breathing, but there was nothing wrong with me?

"Thank you, Doctor. That sounds like great news, but I'm confused. If there's nothing wrong with me, why do I have this awful pain and difficulty breathing?"

The doctor smiled a slow, indifferent smile as he looked up from the chart and directly at me.

"I don't know why your chest hurts and you're short of breath. My job within this Emergency Room is to quickly evaluate you and make sure that you're stable. Your tests all show that there's nothing wrong with you. I'd suggest that you now follow up with your cardiologist and do some additional testing. My work here is done. You're stable and good to go home."

David and I left and headed home. I was embarrassed, concerned, and quite confused. I'd never been to an emergency room before. How was it that I was clearly having a major issue, yet the doctor and tests showed that there was nothing wrong with me? This made no sense. I set up my follow-up appointment with Dr. Taschner and pondered the events that had just unfolded.

At this point in time, health care in the United States was not designed to solve the core reason of people's ill health; the system was paid to repair you after you got sick. Doctors would analyze the symptoms and work to resolve them. Health care focused on particular ailments versus looking at the whole person within their environment. Before this terrifying experience with the chest pain, I hadn't realized this was how the system worked. The emergency room doctor was absolutely correct; technically, there was nothing medically wrong with me.

What I did not understand was that this experience officially began my five-year journey of discovery. It started the evolution of uncovering the root cause of all of my seemingly unrelated health issues that had plagued me my entire life. Chronic eczema, constipation, ovarian cancer, irritable bowel syndrome, colon resection, Crohn's disease. . . the list goes on. By pausing for a moment and taking a look at myself as a whole person within my environment, I discovered a different truth all together.

WHOLE FOOD

LATE NOVEMBER 2014

About two weeks after my surprise visit to the emergency room, I was feeling much better, and the pain in my chest had reduced to a dull ache. I continued to contemplate what might have been the cause to this sudden, alarming pain. Was it indigestion from devouring that late-night pizza? Was it from not getting enough sleep and pushing myself too hard? Despite being unsure, what I was certain of was my desire to gain clarity as to *why* this had happened.

I proceeded to the scheduled appointment with my cardiologist to follow up and further explore what might have caused my chest pain. Dr. Taschner was a passionate leader in our community. He modeled self-care and health, and I was thankful for the opportunity to work with him on my own health. He charted a plan that included a stress test and wearing a heart monitor for a few days to capture any potential unusual rhythms. I felt seen and cared for. As we were wrapping up my office visit, our conversation turned to one about lifestyle.

Dr. Taschner asked, "Have you ever heard of *The China Study*?"

Unsure to what he was referring, I replied honestly. "I have not."

"I'm reading it now, and it's very interesting. It's written by Dr. T. Colin Campbell, and it dives into a study that an emperor of China ordered when he came down with cancer. It seems that it proves that lifestyle and what you eat causes disease."

Now that seemed like absurd information. How could what you eat cause disease?

"That's interesting. I haven't heard of it, but I'll pick up a copy and check it out. Thanks for sharing."

We said our goodbyes, and off I went.

When I got home, I did order a copy of *The China Study*. It arrived a few days later, and I cracked it open. As an avid reader who loved to learn, I was excited to see what discovery this book might have for me.

I only made it a few chapters in. This book was written by a PhD, for other PhDs. Wow. It was painful for me to try to mitigate and comprehend. I tried and I tried, but it was simply too difficult for me to digest. Discouraged but still curious, I instead ordered a DVD co-authored by the same man, this one called *Forks Over Knives*. Perhaps this could be something that would resonate more with me.

And resonate it did. This documentary hit home, and as David and I absorbed it, light bulbs started to go off for us. This was crazy information, but it all made perfect sense. Our standard American diet of chemicals and man-made "food" were not the fuel our bodies were designed to ingest. Eating fatty, hormone-laced meat multiple times a day was not how our tribal ancestors consumed food, and it was making me sick. How did I not know any of this information? Why was no one telling me that what I ate directly affected my health? I was consuming virtually no fiber and definitely nowhere near enough vitamins, minerals, and nutrients. My daily diet of pop-tarts and diet coke were not what God had in mind when designing my body. This newfound information was incredibly disruptive, shifting the course of my life onto a pathway to better understanding my health and wellbeing.

UNCHARTED WATERS

———

SPRING 2015

I was nose down, fingers flying on the keyboard, adrenaline pumping through my veins. I loved my job as a fundraiser, working with incredible, generous donors to build a $240 million Children's Hospital. What I loved even more, though, was my side project; I was raising money to support an "Optimal Healing Environment" at one of our acute care campuses. This was my true passion, both personally and professionally. It lit me up to dive deeper into the awareness that lifestyle was the actual key to optimal wellbeing. I was in charge of my own health. What I ate affected all of me. Food, physical activity, stress, sleep, mental health and knowing our purpose all interconnected to make us a whole, unique person. My passion was palatable and contagious.

I worked away at my desk feeling blessed. I was thriving, satiated, and happy. As I typed away on my computer, scurrying from emails to data base to content reading, my office phone rang.

I hate the phone. Please, email me if you have something to share. Text me if it's emergent. But please, don't call me. Usually, I just ignore a ringing phone, but for some strange reason, I stopped typing and reached for the receiver.

I picked up the phone, placed it up to my ear and mouth, and let out an exasperated "I can't believe you're calling me, I'm deeply inconvenienced" sigh. Then I heard myself say, "Hello."

I didn't say, "Hi, thank you for calling!" or "This is Christin, how may I help you?"—something more approachable, appreciative, or professional. Nope. I clearly let the caller know that I wasn't pleased to be hearing from them during my deep and expansive exhalation and two syllable "Hell-o?"

I have to give credit to this mystery caller; she handled my distain like a champ.

"Hi, is this Christin Collins? My name is _____, and I'm a recruiter. We're doing a national search for an executive fundraising position, and your name came up as a potential candidate. I'm calling today to see if you would have any interest in exploring this further?"

Through the telephone, I was sure she could feel the heat steaming off my face. My complete lack of professionalism was not the way to start a relationship with anyone, never mind a recruiter. I did my darndest to recover from my aloof rudeness. I replied,

"Wow, I'm humbled and honored! Thank you so much for reaching out. I'm actually not interested in exploring any outside opportunities. I absolutely love my job, but I'm deeply moved that my name came up. I truly appreciate your inquiry."

We exchanged pleasantries, and she asked if I thought of anyone who might be a fit to please give her a call. I was about to hang up the receiver, then a thought popped into my mind.

"By the way, may I ask what organization this role is with?"

"Sure, it's with Planned Parenthood."

It was as if time instantly stopped.

I sat, pretty sure I forgot how to breathe, and just let that land. How interesting. I hadn't thought about Planned Parenthood in over twenty years, since I left the Northeast and moved to Florida. How ironic.

"Wow, that's so interesting. Planned Parenthood actually saved my life."

Now it was the recruiters turn to be stunned. We went on to have a thirty-minute conversation discussing my experience with the health care provider and the unique circumstances of my journey with them. As a result, we decided to keep our conversation going, and I would explore the role that she was recruiting for.

A few months later, after much research, many conversations, and intense negotiation, I accepted the role. I was the perfect person to shed light on all of the vital care that this group provided, including to seemingly normal middle-class folks who are uninsured or underinsured. An overwhelming number of friends and family tried to talk me out of accepting this position due to the controversies that seemed to plague the organization. They felt it was professional suicide. Yet, I had a few girlfriends who were thrilled with the prospect of me taking this on, as they, too, had life changing experiences with this organization. I felt a surreal calm as I moved toward this change and embraced the unique circumstances that made this an exceptional fit for a new chapter.

The final details were coming together as I flew home from a women's leadership conference in San Diego. I'd be heading out to the Bahamas twelve hours later for a much-needed week of vacation. As I flew across the country, digesting this new opportunity, I gladly accepted a glass of wine from the flight attendant, and typed up my resignation letter. Tears silently streamed down my face as I reflected on my five-year journey with the hospital. I thought of all the incredibly generous donors and colleagues I'd been forever blessed to cross paths with.

I would miss them, but I knew the hardest part of this change would be leaving behind the work that was happening under the leadership of Scott Kashman. I had transformed so much from our shared experiences, growing in knowledge and awareness that lifestyle was medicine. It had become abundantly clear that how we were managing our health was not working. Word was spreading, and it was exciting. There were a small but steady swell of others who began listening, co-creating, and transcending. We were the outlying misfits for sure, but we were a band of warriors who were doing transformative, innovative work. I cherished it and was going to miss this part of my role more than my heart could handle.

Scott was the only colleague who knew of my recruitment call and the months of exploration and negotiation that followed. In true servant-leadership style, he actually helped me re-write my resume, proofread my emails, and mock interviewed me. He even helped me negotiate my new contract. Never once did he try to dissuade me. We both knew that the work he and I were passionately creating would be more difficult to move forward with upon my departure, yet there were no guilty moments and not a stitch of selfishness. Just true, foundational friendship that supported my exploration and ultimately led me to success.

As I landed back in southwest Florida after my time in San Diego, I sent Scott a text to let him know that the deal had come together and that I had verbally accepted the new role. He texted back joyful celebration, and asked when I would be letting our health care system know. As I was heading out of the country in twelve hours and would have no internet or phone connection for the next seven days, I relayed that I would share the news upon my return next week. It really was not going to make any difference to the system or to the team.

Scott agreed, yet asked if in confidence he could share this news with our CEO. As we knew my departure would impact our existing work, he felt it would be helpful to reach out to our leader and help Scott continue his work. Yes, I told him that he could confidentially share this news with our CEO.

"But please, keep it under wraps."

Bright and early the following morning, David and I set out to the Bahamas with another fun couple. We looked forward to spending a week on a boat floating around at sea, sipping delicious cocktails, and eating fresh, local food. We took naps and dove into the crystal-clear water. Our skin was getting darker, and the quiet of the waves hitting the boat lulled me into a state of tranquility.

Cut off from the outer world, there was a lot of time to contemplate. We discussed my past five years with the system and the successes that I experienced. It was a bit scary to think about starting something new—especially such a big role for a controversial organization. It was an incredible leadership opportunity that uniquely fit with who I was. I embraced the sadness of leaving the pioneering work with Scott and gave thanks for having the opportunity to have worked together.

The days flew by, and suddenly it was the second to last day of our excursion in the Bahamas. Instead of spending the night "on the hook," our boat pulled up to shore and docked at a marina. It was different to have access to land, as well as to cell service. My plan was to have absolutely no connection with the outside world this entire week, but it was hard to fight the urge to connect and see what was happening with the rest of the planet. I decided to stay the course and remain unplugged—that is, until a few hours and a few cocktails later.

We were enjoying an incredibly fun Bahamian pub crawl, where the mixture of sun, sand, and rum were making me feel on top of the world. I headed into a lady's room, and for some reason brought my cell phone with me. I believe I justified it by thinking I'd taking pictures along the way. As I sat to pee, I stared at my phone.

Don't do it. You've been doing so good! Two more days. Stay strong.

I couldn't help myself. Something made me switch off airplane mode. I had conjured up some excuse in my head that my stepdaughter might need me, so perhaps I should just turn it on for a hot second to make sure she was ok. That was a hilarious thought, as *she* has been taking care of *me* since she was five.

As airplane mode was switched off, it was as if my phone was having a seizure. I swear it was physically shaking. Red dots were popping up everywhere, and the numbers were indicating communications in the hundreds. I laughed! Looks like I was going to have my work cut out for me when I returned home. I scrolled quickly through my work emails, and noticed there were multiple outreaches from Scott.

That's weird. He knows I'm away. He knows I don't have phone access. I hope everything's okay.

Then I scroll through my texts.

More from Scott.

"PLEASE CALL ME."

I wasn't sure at this point how international texting, emailing, or calling worked, but what I did know from my days as a flight attendant was that no matter which mode you selected, it was expensive. My phone was supposed to be off. As my head cleared, I quickly reactivated airplane mode, then hurried back to reconnect with David. I tried to digest the seemingly emergent outreach from Scott, but then convinced myself that he was fine. My thoughts ping-ponged back and forth, weighing on me.

David noticed I was a bit frazzled upon my return and asked if everything was alright. I didn't share my cell phone indiscretion, and concentrated on the Bahamian music that was flowing and the fresh cocktail that David had ordered for me. Life was amazing, and everything unfolding at home could wait.

Except, it couldn't. I couldn't stop thinking about why Scott had reached out. It began eating away at me, especially since he was so instrumental in helping me land the new job. I wasn't being fair, and I needed to reply to his communications.

It was confession time. I shared with David that I had switched on my phone and that there was some communication from back home that might need my immediate attention. David educated me that my decision to connect from a phone that did not have an international plan was incredibly expensive. (Yes, those ninety seconds ended up costing me $240. I'm not kidding.) He agreed to help me call home the next morning from the dock, using the marina Wi-Fi, not my phone plan. The rest of the trip became a whirlwind.

We called Scott bright and early the following morning, and thankfully he answered. He asked if I had signed the documents with Planned Parenthood yet. I hadn't, as my home printer wasn't working when I landed from San Diego, and I hadn't had time to figure all of that out during my twelve-hour turnaround. I had emailed my acceptance and verbally gave it to them, but I hadn't signed.

"Oh, that's awesome!" he said.

Awesome? What's awesome? What are you talking about? You helped me land this job...

"As you gave me permission to do, I told our CEO you were going to be leaving. His reaction was the same as mine—that this would be a huge loss for the system and would disrupt the health and wellness work that we were just beginning to get off the ground. I asked if I could take you on my team in the system so that we could work on health and wellness full-time. We would be creating this opportunity. Would you consider staying and taking on this role?"

Mind you, I'm sitting on the front of a forty-four foot yacht in the Bahamas. Beautiful boats lined up in their marina slips. Glorious sunshine beat down. Birds flew carefree overhead. I could smell the clean ocean water. I felt like I was watching a movie.

What are you talking about, Scott Kashman? Don't you dare do this to me. After four months of conversation, interviewing, negotiating, and accepting, you throw this at me? I've moved on. I gave them my word. It was a leadership role with a nationally established organization that saved my life. There was room for me to grow professionally there. I was passionate

*about their work. I'd made my decision. Please don't take
me out of this relaxed, surreal moment and completely blow
my mind.*

"Scott, creating a niche where you can work on health and
wellness full-time is great news, but we both know that most
medical professionals don't embrace this method, nor is it
how the system works. Plus, it would take months to get
this position approved. Nothing happens fast in health care."

His response stunned me. In the past five days—of which two
were weekend days—the system had moved forward with
creating this role. They pulled together Scott, the CEO, the
COO, and the head of HR within seventy-two hours and had
approved a position to innovate health and wellness.

Breathless, I thanked Scott for letting me know. I promised
to reach back out in forty-eight hours when I returned to the
US. I sat in complete shock and took it all in. *Now what? Was
this for real?* Nothing moved fast in health care, yet suddenly
my dream opportunity while working with my dream boss
was right in front of me. But I'd already moved on. I'd already
said yes. Plus, this newly created role was risky. The vast
majority of providers didn't embrace lifestyle as medicine
and actually felt threatened by this work. I'd be crazy to take
this on. There were already enough targets on my back from
the work I'd been doing under the radar; this would take the
resistance to a whole new level.

The stirring behind me brought me back into the moment.
David had joined me on the front of the boat and sat down
beside me. He placed his caring arm around my shoulders

and asked if everything was okay back home. I thanked him for helping me connect and shared the news. Now, it was his turn to sit quietly. He took the news in, knowing how uncommon it was for something of this magnitude to happen so fast. It spoke volumes to both of us without the need for another spoken word.

Instead, we watched the boat captain untie us from the dock and we sailed away back into uncharted waters.

SYSTEM DIRECTOR HEALTH & WELLNESS

JULY 2015

Clarity came over me like a tidal wave, waking me up abruptly in the middle of the night. It caused me to sit up so fast that I nearly smashed my head into the low-clearance ceiling on the boat's rather small bed. David lay sound asleep next to me, unaware of my newfound knowing. I finally had my answer, just in time. For the past forty-eight hours, I had been tormented with the new information that Scott had shared. Obsessed and unable to let go, how would I move forward?

I had already said yes to Planned Parenthood. It was an amazing opportunity that completely aligned with my passion. It was total career advancement with lots of room to grow. We had come to an agreement, and I had accepted. My word was all I had.

But at the same time, I loved the work I was co-creating with Scott and the others who knew that lifestyle was truly the foundation for wellbeing. We were like undercover agents, making head way in this field without too much attention or conflict. With this new opportunity, we'd be able to do our work above the radar. Full-time. Out in the open. Plus, I'd be working with my mentor who created a work environment in which I thrived. Dream job, dream boss, and national leadership.

But I had already said yes to Planned Parenthood.

All things equal, I would stay. Of course I would stay. I was here on this planet to do this work with Scott. We were both complete misfits, in sync and perfectly aligned. We completed each other's sentences. He understood me and I understood him. He brought out the best in me and I brought out the best in him. Along with a few other fellow misfit colleagues, we'd be able to actually pioneer this work and turn it into a national best practice. It was now so clear. All things equal, I would stay.

If only life were that simple.

The next few weeks after returning home were a continuous roller coaster ride as I navigated conversations with the recruiter, explaining my sudden change of plans. This role still had to be posted internally. I went through the job posting and interview process with the health care system, for a role that was not yet defined. Most of all, it became apparent that all things were not equal. Staying would give me a significant financial cut, as well as no clear path for career growth or advancement. Our family was still working to fiscally recover from the great recession of 2008 which had deeply impacted us. Every dollar counted. I was more confused than ever, sick to my stomach as I felt a deep responsibility to both companies.

Finally, it was decision time. The hospital had offered me the new role. Planned Parenthood had patiently waited while I decided. David and I sat down at our kitchen table, and he shared his thoughts on how I should move forward.

"Babe, you should stay with Lee Health. You should stay and work with Scott. You guys are co-creating incredible, vital work that will help millions of lives. Your partnership is a rare combination. You should stay and continue to grow it."

As I absorbed his words, my heart pumped out of my chest. David never, ever ceased to surprise me, and this time was no exception. My husband, the finance guy, just told me to stay and do the work I was born to do instead of following the money and potential career expansion. Stay. Follow my purpose.

And staying is exactly what I did. Over the next few years, our team became nationally recognized for our work in health and wellbeing. Dr. Sal, my executive partner, became a board member with the American College of Lifestyle Medicine and a national leader in lifestyle medicine. Our team presented at ACLM's national conference, twice. Our National Speaker Series brought in world renowned speakers, touching tens of thousands of lives. Our latest speaker was the one and only Dr. Deepak Chopra.

I was blessed to write a chapter in Scott's book, *Mindful Healthcare*, which outlined the history of how we built The Optimal Healing Environment. We won the Baldridge-inspired Governor's Sterling Award for this work, being the first community hospital in the state of Florida to do so. We created integrated, innovative destination spaces for people to come together, work out, be educated, heal, and connect. We brought mindfulness to the forefront of health, showcasing the importance of the mind-body connection. The list of our achievements went on.

Yes, I stayed. The road was full of twists and turns, trials and tribulations. We faced many obstacles and changes in leadership. We experienced providers who venomously disagreed with our belief that lifestyle was medicine. Still, it was one of the greatest chapters of my life thus far. I grew so much doing this pioneering work, of which the true impact would not be realized for years to come. It taught me to be true to my beliefs and my own journey and to cast my vision and go for it, unattached to the outcomes. Most importantly, it also taught me to gracefully walk away when it was time to go.

THE WELLNESS WHEEL

———

WINTER 2015

Scott and I gathered in his office for our monthly meeting. He was the greatest boss; he left me alone to do my work while being available to listen and support me when needed. My autonomy left me room to create and grow, yet the opportunity to collaborate with him created a haven for deep thinking and problem solving. His style of leadership really worked for me. While the work we did was incredibly challenging, I was inspired to keep going and figure out how to promote keeping people from getting sick versus just repairing them afterwards. I looked forward to this one hour meeting each month, as it often proved to spark new discoveries and set me on an exciting path for the next thirty days.

There were leaders in the system who were not in agreement with our work. They felt that we were just vegetable pushers—too extreme in our passion for plant-based living. Both my family and Scott's had changed our diets to vegan and were having transformative experiences. We were usually the outliers at lunch meetings and events, the weirdos who would bring our own food and not partake in the processed ham and cheese subs provided. We didn't make a big deal out of it, but it clearly displeased some people around us. We were different, and different can make some uncomfortable.

"Christin, I'm receiving feedback that our messaging and programs are too pushy. It's being perceived that our wellness work is only about becoming a vegan. Some executives are questioning where we're steering things."

My eyes roll to the back of my head. I found bureaucracy incredibly frustrating. Have they watched *Forks Over Knives*? Have they taken the Complete Health Improvement Program (CHIP)? Do they look at the science or attend the American College of Lifestyle Medicine conference? These things had changed my life. Why had they not changed theirs?

"Scott, that's absolutely ridiculous. It's not just about eating vegetables. Yes, vegetables are very important, but like the teachings from CHIP, it's so much more than that."

David and I had enrolled in CHIP the year prior after my unexplainable health scare. It was offered to Lee Health employees thanks to Scott, and was an incredible journey that helped educate us about the different components of our lifestyle that affect our health. We gathered as a small group twice a week for three months, sampling plant-based recipes, watching informative videos, and discussing weekly readings. The transformations that people experienced in this program were magical. Chronic diseases reversed. Pounds fell off. Skin began to glow. Energy skyrocketed. People got their groove back.

"I'm just sharing with you the feedback I'm receiving. We need to better understand it, and adjust our messaging so that we don't come across as being all about vegetables."

Still extremely frustrated, I engaged. "Well, it's not only about eating vegetables."

Scott smirked, knowing he was successfully under my skin.

"Okay, then what else is it about?"

Exasperated, I spew back, "Well, it's also about physical activity, stress, sleep, mental health, and knowing your why."

I wasn't sure where that came from, but I was impressed with my response, especially with how concise it was, and the confidence with which I delivered it. How silly were people to not understand this? Isn't it obvious to everyone?

"Interesting. Thanks for sharing that. Could you please walk me through those points again?"

This time, Scott had pen in hand. I was not 100 percent sure I could repeat what I'd just said, but I hoped for the best as I started to speak.

"Yes. Besides eating vegetables, people need to engage in physical activity. They can't just sit on their butts all day. They need to get enough sleep to rejuvenate, reduce stress, support their mental health, and know their why."

In typical Kashman style, Scott scribbled furiously. He paused, looked up from his messy notes, and asked:

"What do you mean, 'Know their why?'"

Excellent question. I'm not sure how that one popped up, but I'd never give him that satisfaction.

"You know. . . know their *why*. What's their point? What's their purpose? Why do they bother getting out of bed each morning? What is their reason to live?"

And with that, the Wellness Wheel was born. We would spend the next year researching these six spokes, deciding if they were the right guiding principles for health and well-being. Some wanted to remove mental health. Others wanted to add in smoking cessation. Ultimately, we landed back on the original six. They became the lens we would use to guide our work, showcasing their interconnectivity to our overall wellbeing. If one spoke of the wheel was off, they were all off.

I began exploring each of these spokes personally as well as professionally. Nutrition and physical activity were most tangible for me to embrace and dive into, while the seeds regarding sleep, stress, mental health, and purpose had been sown but yet to be fully understood.

IN THE STATE OF INFLAMMATION

———

SPRING 2016

As my journey of health and wellbeing unfolded, I continued to explore ways to better understand my body and how my lifestyle was affecting it. At this point, I was a vegan triathlete, but I was still experiencing brain fog, fatigue, and chronic distention of my midsection most afternoons. Personally and professionally, I knew all bodies had little things that don't always work right, but I was really aiming for optimal health and wanted to know how to get there.

I decided to order an extensive, all-encompassing blood work-up of my markers. This testing included things like hormones, vitamins, inflammation, and lipids, totaling one hundred different measurements. The results would help fine tune my eating and set a strong baseline to continue gauging my development.

A few weeks after my blood draw, the test results arrived in the mail. It was a hefty stack of paperwork filled with charts and graphs. I definitely felt well examined. I was set to have a call the following day to connect with my doctor and walk through the detailed results.

The next day, as Dr. Sal walked us through each page, he expressed that my markers were looking excellent. This was a huge relief for me. Apparently, all of those green smoothies were paying off!

Dr. Sal and I both continued to look at the report in front of each of us. Once we got to the inflammation graph, it was just a single horizontal line that started and ended about a half inch from each side of the page, seemingly identical to the other graphs in the report. The measurement usually showed as a vertical dash somewhere on the horizontal line, indicating if your results are within a normal range, low or high. In this particular case, there was not a dash on the horizontal line.

"That's odd," he stated, which isn't exactly what you want to hear from your physician.

"What's odd, Dr. Sal?"

"For some reason, they didn't test your inflammation. I requested that information, but for some reason they didn't test for it."

Now, I was a little worried. *That* is *weird. They tested about a hundred markers, yet they decided not to run this one particular test. How did they miss it? Why did they miss it?*

Something felt off that they would skip over one specific little marker.

I began settling into the reality that the lab simply forgot to measure my inflammation. Just as I was about to give up and ask Dr. Sal to move on with his assessment, he found the detail on my charts that would change everything.

"Hang on. Look way over to the right side of the paper. Almost off the page. See that little black dash off the graph, almost off the paper? There's the marker. Your inflammation measures well over 100 percent."

A very clear thought immediately soared through my mind.

In the state of inflammation, disease is created.

I heard it again.

In the state of inflammation, disease is created.

I was a vegan triathlete. My blood work was exceptional, as was my body weight and overall health. Why would my inflammation literally be off the chart? My heart was racing in my chest, as I knew this was very emergent information. I looked healthy. Outside of being tired and having my tummy inflate most afternoons, I felt healthy. Why was this happening?

This was the moment I became even more aware that traditional medicine might not hold the answers I was searching for. I followed the rules; I ate clean, exercised regularly, didn't smoke, and drank moderately. I should've been the picture of overall health! But, here I was with an extreme amount of inflammation. The implications haunted me.

In the state of inflammation, disease is created.

I needed to figure out why my inflammation was off the chart.

GRAM

Stephanie, the Downtown Diva, was a hippy-chic, bohemian, glamourous influencer who represented all things chic about urban living. She was an actress, a freelance journalist, a community volunteer, and a trendsetter. I had first met Stephanie a decade earlier. We were both attending an event at a local school which supported young women and girls who were struggling in traditional school settings. The girls experienced hardships beyond belief, and the organization provided a safe and loving environment for them to heal and grow.

The Diva often attended events around town, snapping photos for the society section of our paper. She also wrote an exciting column for our glam magazine, *Gulfshore Life*. I always looked forward to my monthly copy of this glossy compilation of high society, real estate, fashion, and trends. Her column was my favorite, though, as she stayed true to herself and covered topics and people that some may find a little out there.

Recently, she had written about her experience with Gigi, a local medium. I wasn't sure what a medium was, but the story drew me in right away as Stephanie described her mystical experience. I found it interesting that during her session, she had connected with people who had passed away and that Gigi was able to help her better understand some puzzle pieces that helped Stephanie release some tension and stress. Interesting. Love her for sharing this bizarre experience, but not my cup of tea.

For the next few months, this article popped up in various conversations. At a breakfast meeting for the hospital, someone brought up the story and how healing the Diva's experience seemed to be. At the spa getting my nails done, my nail technician rambled on about her recent visit to Gigi and how transformative it was. Gigi kept coming up in unexpected places.

I began to ponder, *why do I keep hearing about Gigi? As I was always game for new adventures, should I go see her? I'm so incredibly busy with work and preparing to co-chair one of the biggest charity events in our region. It would be ridiculous to take the time to do such a silly thing, never mind spend the money, right?*

The tipping point came when I was at a meeting with a very important woman in our community. She was no joke—straight forward, widely respected, and buttoned up. Before we could begin discussing the business at hand, she shared about her recent visit with Gigi. It was so interesting that she'd just booked a session for her mother.

"This sort of thing didn't interest me at all, but the Diva's article was so funny, I had to try it. I couldn't believe the information that Gigi shared. There's absolutely no way she could've known that stuff about me. I'm still thinking about how she could have possibly accessed the intel!"

I asked her for Gigi's contact information and immediately reached out to book an appointment. Unfortunately, she was booked for the next six months! So, I scheduled an appointment for some random day in February, put it in my calendar, and completely forgot about it.

February rolled around. The charity event I was co-chairing was only days away, and I was very stressed. Between work and this wine festival event, days were flying by and every hour mattered. As I woke up before the sun to sprint through another marathon day, I checked my phone to digest the calendar. What do I have to tackle today?

Most things made sense and were definitely a top priority. Yet, one appointment stood out, and I had no idea what it meant.

Gigi, 2:00 p.m.

Gigi? Who is Gigi? Is this for work or the wine fest?

Slowly, it came back to me. Gigi. *That* Gigi. The medium I had contacted a half year ago. Today was finally the day of my appointment. I found it hilarious. Clearly, I didn't have time to go see a medium today. I'd have to dig out her contact information and cancel.

Yet, I didn't cancel. Something made me stop and contemplate. This woman was impossible to get an appointment with, and I actually had the chance today. The experiences others had shared were super interesting. My curiosity was too powerful. It was my turn to see what Gigi had to say.

That afternoon I connected with Gigi, mentally prepared to keep the straightest face I'd ever kept. There was no way I was going to give her any ammunition with my body language or agreements. She'd have to prove to me that she was truly gaining insights from another realm, not from my nodding or hint dropping.

Gigi didn't disappoint. There was absolutely no way she could know the things she shared. Chills ran up and down my spine as she connected with my deceased Grandmother and lovingly shared stories from my time with her in Connecticut. As I took in her messaging, my heart was pulsating with disbelief and gratitude. How incredible to be reconnected with such a special person who had passed over a decade earlier. Doubt bubbled up in spurts during this experience; *how could it possibly be that Gigi was speaking to Gram right now?*

"Your grandmother wants you to know that everything is going to be all right. Don't worry so much and enjoy the journey."

I stared back at Gigi, not sure what to say or what to think. She continued.

"It's very important to her that you know that everything is okay. She's holding something up like she's toasting you. Was she a drinker? It seems that she's holding up a glass of wine, toasting you. Yes, it's a glass of wine. A glass of red wine."

Gram wasn't a drinker. If memory served me correctly, she and I had never had an alcoholic beverage together while she was alive. Why would she be holding up a glass of red wine?

The Wine Fest! She was referencing this weekend's Wine Fest event. She was telling me that everything was going to be alright.

Remaining still and upright, I didn't respond to Gigi. I wouldn't lead her to any discoveries, and she wouldn't get any feedback from me. While that information was incredibly intuitive, I would remain stoic and not give her any indication that she'd hit a nerve.

"She wants you to know that this is real, and that you can connect with her without me at any time at all. She's constantly guiding you and your family. She watches over you and is so proud of you."

Holding back tears, I continue to remain still and unflinching. I could hear my breathing echoing in my ears. Could this actually be real?

"She's smiling at you, acknowledging how darn stubborn and strong willed you are. She says that when you get back home, your bed isn't going to be made. And how she's laughing! She said that'll do the trick to show you that this is real. She's leaving us now but says that she's always there for you. Access her at any time."

Gigi and I closed out our session and I thanked her for the interesting experience. Not sure what to make of it, I climbed into my car and drove home in a fog. Memories of my grandmother kept coming in and out. It was soothing to think about her love and the possibility that she's watching over us. Ridiculous, yes, but soothing.

Soon I was back home, pulling into my garage. I laughed at the idea that I'd forgotten to make the bed. I *always* made my bed; it was the first thing I did each morning when I got up. I felt disheveled and unkept when my bed was unmade. David was tolerant of this pet peeve, and knew how important this detail was to me. Seventeen years together ensured we always made our bed.

As I entered the house, I made a bee line to the bedroom. Time to squish this insanity. I had work to do. I threw open our bedroom doors, knowing that I would see that same thing I saw every day—our perfectly made bed with the pillows strategically positioned.

When I looked at the bed, my mouth dropped open. The sight knocked the wind out of me. Dizzy with disbelief, I took in the scene. Before me was the messiest unmade bed I'd ever seen. Pillows scattered on the floor. I could see impressions of two sleepy bodies in the sheets, as if David and I were still sleeping there. Clearly, we had made no attempt at all to straighten up this morning. How could this be? We *always* made the bed!

As I regained my composure, I mentally reviewed the morning. *How had I left the house without making my bed?* That was impossible. It was simply a routine I never missed.

Then it hit me. I had left the house super early today when David was still sleeping. Of *course* I didn't make the bed; he was still in it! But, even when I left before him, David would make the bed. He knew investing thirty seconds pulling up the covers and picking up the pillows was a wise use of time. Happy wife, happy life. He never overlooked something this simple. While I couldn't think of an explanation, I couldn't help but giggle that my grandmother reconnected with me over an unmade bed, of all things.

A few hours later, David arrived home. I was in the kitchen making dinner and drinking a glass of red wine. Before I could say anything, he kissed me hello and shared,

"Hi, honey. Dinner smells delicious. Hey, I'm so sorry I didn't have time to make the bed this morning. I got a call that a client was sitting in my office and wanted to meet with me, so I flew out of here like a crazy person. I felt really bad about not making the bed, because I know how important that is to you. I hope you aren't mad at me!"

I continued to stir the pot on the stove. A slow smile grew on my face.

Gram, you devil you. Of all the ways you could've show me your spirit was with me always, you chose an unmade bed. Classic.

I picked up the bottle of red wine that I had opened for this special occasion. Pouring David a glass, I held up mine for a secret toast.

"Babe, you don't have to apologize. Sometimes a break in routine shakes things up. I love you. And everything is going to be alright."

PART 3

THE INNER WORK

THE DIVA

——

LATE FEBRUARY 2017

Wine Fest was a smashing success. The generosity of our community was breathtaking, and we raised millions of dollars to support the mental health and wellbeing of children in our region. Florida was the least funded state in the nation when it came to mental health programs and services for kids. On top of that, our county was the least funded county in Florida. We were the worst of the worst. After a year of spreading this message and rallying support to address this inequity, our community came together to begin to work to change that. I was exhausted, but incredibly grateful and inspired.

A week after this festival, I was at a local hotel ballroom greeting guests as they entered another fundraiser. This one was for Planned Parenthood. My recent revisit with this organization had stirred something long dormant inside of me. I was sad not to have taken the position with them, so I knew I still wanted to support them in some capacity. It became clear that sharing my story with others might spread awareness of their impact on overall health. I offered to tell my story if it would be useful. This day, I was the keynote speaker at their annual Lee County lunch.

Nervous but excited, I stood in the entryway and welcomed guests. Suddenly from around the corner, I felt an energy entering the space before a physical body appeared. Knowing someone was coming around the bend, I waited with antici-pation to see who else was coming to this lunch. The people in our neck of the woods didn't wildly support Planned Parent-hood, so I wasn't sure if I was about to encounter friend or foe.

Before I knew it, the Diva appeared in front of me. As usual, she was a collection of grace, glamour, a pinch of hesita-tion, and a big, beautiful smile. I hadn't seen her in months, and it always warmed my heart to connect with her. Mem-ories of my recent visit with Gigi washed over me, and I couldn't wait to thank her for writing the article about this talented medium.

"Hey, Steph! So great to see you! I wanted to thank you... Last week I finally went to go see Gigi. Wow, what a trip. She was spot on. It was such a cool experience."

Stephanie paused, gave me a big hug, and continued walking into the ballroom. After a few steps passed, she looked back at me over her shoulder with a coy reply.

"If you think Gigi was good, wait until you read this month's column."

I hadn't had a moment to crack open this month's *Gulfshore Life Magazine*, so as soon as I returned home that afternoon,

I found my copy on our coffee table. I feverishly turned the pages to get to Stephanie's column. As promised, this month she recounted her experience with a woman in Naples who took her through a past life regression. Deciding I wasn't going to wait nine months to try this modality out, I immediately called the woman and was surprised when she answered the phone.

"Hi, my name is Christin Collins. I'm friends with the Diva. I just ran into her today and read her article about the past life regression. I would love to have one!"

Clearly, I wasn't the first person who had called after reading the column. Carolyn was welcoming and kind as she giggled at my enthusiasm.

"Well, thank you for calling. Yes, Stephanie's article has created quite the buzz. I'm rather booked up, but I just hung up with someone that needed to cancel their appointment on Thursday. I realize that's short notice, but if you're available, I'd be happy to see you."

It was already Tuesday. My weeks were slammed, but I wasn't going to pass up the opportunity to try this out even if it meant shuffling some stuff around.

"I'll be there. This is so exciting! Is there anything I need to do over the next forty-eight hours to prepare?"

I couldn't believe this was happening so fast. It must have been meant to be!

"Not a thing. I look forward to seeing you Thursday."

Two days later, I set off for Naples. I had not shared with anyone my recent experience with Gigi, nor had I chosen to share about my appointment with Carolyn. This was some weird stuff I was dabbling in, and I wasn't interested in receiving others' judgment. This would be my own private dabbling, as I was really only in it for the fun and adventure!

Carolyn met me at the door with a warm greeting.

"It's so nice to meet you. Please have a seat. Here's some paperwork I need you to fill out. Once you're done, I'll review it, then we can get to work."

Simple enough. I sat down with the paperwork, freely answering the posed questions. I was honest and transparent—almost flippant. If she wanted to know these things about my life, then sure, I would tell her. They weren't necessarily things I freely shared, and I couldn't see their connection to past life regression, but what the heck.

I handed the completed forms back to Carolyn, and she began to read them over. I squirmed a little in my chair, as I had let it all hang out when I truthfully answered her inquiries. Hoping I hadn't made a mistake by choosing to do so, I waited with anticipation for her response. Finally, she looked up from the paperwork and spoke.

"Well, thank you for your honest answers. I have to be honest with you. I don't think we should do a past life regression at this time. You have some *this life-time* work that needs to be addressed first."

Oh, here we go. Multiple sessions. Let me guess, she wants to sell me a package. This is another sales tool to get my money. Why is it that so many people are scams?

Before I answered her with, "Thanks but no thanks," I noticed picture frames above her desk. There were certificates showing her education, and many of them. And they weren't from made up, woo woo institutions. They were all reputable, well known schools with fancy degrees and titles. Maybe she wasn't a fraud after all.

"Okay. I might be open to that. Let me ask, how many sessions do you think I would need before I could get to the past life stuff?"

Carolyn smiled, with just a hint of amusement lighting up her eyes.

"Well, that will depend on you. The more open you are, the faster it happens. Everyone is different. I suspect, based on the openness you expressed on your form, that you're ready to do this work."

I'd already done this work. As a young adult, I'd spent years in therapy working through the dark experiences from my youth. This work threaded through my marriages and my capacity to love and be loved. It had been years since these traumas occurred, yet Carolyn felt there was a need to revisit them. I wasn't pleased, as my past didn't define me. However, my intuition told me to embrace the advice of the expert and begin where she suggested.

And with that, we began my first hypnotherapy session. I'd never heard of hypnotherapy before but was immediately intrigued by the experience and the science behind it. I ended up doing a half dozen sessions with Carolyn because I wanted to, not because *she* wanted me to. It was an incredible rewiring of my defaults and opened me up to heal past wounds. When we did get to a past life session, things began to make sense. I was thankful we'd taken the time to work through things the way Carolyn suggested.

At the same time, I wasn't exactly sure what to make of it or how much to believe. Like my experience with Gigi, this was all very foreign to me. Yet, I was feeling so much better, lighter, and calmer. The contrast I was experiencing between wellness within traditional health care and these new modalities began to become evident. My stomach aches, skin irritations, headaches, and energy were all improving, and it wasn't because of modern medicine.

ROOT CAUSE

———

FALL 1972

From the outside, it all seemed so normal.

Complete middle class, white suburbia.

Father with his PhD teaching at a local college.

Mom raising two kids with a flexible secretarial job, organizing carpools, and leading my Brownie Troop.

Two towheaded kids involved in school with many extra activities from dance to football.

A shoreline home that was forever undergoing work and improvements.

Church on Sunday.

A solid neighborhood where tag and street wiffle ball often blessed the afternoon air.

My neighborhood was the poster for the American Dream, or so it seemed. Similar to how I could never truly know the journey of the passengers on a plane, things are often not as they appear.

I remember the first day I sensed something was off. It was nothing overt that should have raised screeching sirens or screams, but I vividly remember the feeling inside of five-and-a-half-year-old me, knowing that the way he placed me on his lap and held me there felt invasive.

We were on a family trip, out of town visiting a family with whom we annually got together. We sat in the family room, two sets of parents and some kids, and hung around, talked, and played. I'm not sure what prompted it, but he picked me up from what I was doing and placed me on his lap. It felt *off*, too close, and intuitively inappropriate, though nothing brazen to declare.

His hands were on either side of my shoulders, holding me in place. I sat there, still. Very, very still. I could feel his breath on the back of my neck, and I wanted to move so bad, but I sat. I was a good girl. We were in a room full of people, and I didn't want to upset anyone or make a scene. These were friends and family, so I would behave. But this was the marked beginning of much, much trauma.

I would sustain over a decade of abuse from a person who was supposed to protect me. Love me above all else. Show me the world. Treat me like a princess. Help me achieve anything and everything. But this would not be my experience. Life should be full of chicken pot pie, getting help with homework, baseball games, and picnics at the beach. Instead, my seemingly middle-class childhood was one of immense pain, fear, confusion, devastation, and sorrow.

I've spent my entire life since this first memory recovering from the childhood I experienced and finding my way back to me.

When I started dating, I worked diligently to stay emotionally unattached, never allowing someone deep into my heart. I constantly worked to control my environments, steering clear of situations that might not provide anticipated outcomes. Since grade school, I was forever distracted from the present moment. On each quarterly report card, every single class provided the feedback "Talks too much" in the comment section.

In hindsight, I didn't have an attention disorder, I had an *"I'm too scared to be still and in the moment"* disorder.

These threads continued through my romantic relationships, my family, my health, my professional life. . . you name it, it was underlying. Yet, it took almost fifty years to understand how it all connected. Doing the work to face, embrace, exhale, and heal would be my way out of the vicious cycle.

MANIFESTING
MY REALITY

FEBRUARY 2018

I'm not sure how it happened, but I was carrying $33,000 of debt on my American Express card. I made plenty of money, and wasn't even responsible for that much of my household carrying costs. Yet, somehow, at the ripe age of fifty-one, I found myself in debt, *again*. It suffocated me. It kept me up at night. It made me sick, scared, and sad. It was a constant weight to carry around, enveloping me any time I tried to be present and still.

The debt was only half of the problem. Each month, I would play games with the credit card in an attempt to manage this weight. This entailed buying items and returning them so I didn't pay interest on the debt. As you can imagine, it was exhausting to constantly buy and return that much stuff, month after month. It made me sad and stressed out. Ironically, that still wasn't the real problem.

My amazing husband, David, had been a very successful banker since the day I met him two decades earlier. He was excellent with money and was very generous in sharing it with me, our family, and many charities. When we first met, I was in debt. He patiently and kindly coached me, helping to create a plan to reduce my debt. This included educating me as to why debt was such a pile of quicksand. He didn't *save* me by paying off the debt directly. Instead, he provided me a home, food, and a plan to help me pay off my own debt. This would take two years of teaching me money managing skills which, somehow, I'd never acquired. When I finally paid my debt off, we celebrated the release of this baggage. I was very grateful, and vowed to never put myself in that position again.

Two years later, David and I were engaged to be married. In this loving merger, we decided to keep our financials separate. He was entering our marriage with a number of assets, a high-paying job, and most importantly, two beautiful children that he loved taking care of. I was entering with a low-paying job, champagne taste, and no assets. To be fair, we both felt it best not to co-mingle assets. David provided us our lifestyle, and I was to take care of my spending above and beyond our living expenses—you know, things like my 5 series BMW that I clearly didn't need, my weekly nail appointment, and other key essentials that I would splurge on. Managing things in this way kept us from disagreeing on how we should spend our money. There was only one request from David to move forward with this: I was to promise that I would never, ever put myself in debt again.

I was successful at this for the first fifteen years. Ironically, my credit card balance started creeping up as I approached my fifties and was making the most money I had ever made. At first, it was a thousand rolling over each month, then a few thousand, until about two years later, it became $33,000.

I couldn't ignore it anymore. It was eating my insides, and hiding it from him made my heart hurt. I felt horrible that I had broken my promise to David and myself. Frustrated and truly unsure of how it had happened, I decided it was time to focus; it was time to manifest this debt disappearing in the next four months. I wasn't going to be attached to *how* it disappeared. I was just going to concentrate on the feeling that the credit card balance was nonexistent. I had received random surprise checks in the mail before, and this would be the opportune time for it to happen again!

I'd watched the documentary *The Secret* a decade earlier, but hadn't thought about it for years. During this period of desperation, it crossed my mind again. As it suggests, I would try to *feel* what it feels like to be debt free, and put it out there that I *am* debt free. We attract what we project. I was on my knees, desperate to make this go away. I would try anything.

I set a date for this manifestation: March 31. Each day, I would run to the mailbox to see if a $33,000 check miraculously arrived in the mail, but my manifestation power didn't seem to be working. As the date crept closer, my spirit began to wane. I took no other action to alleviate this debt. I just concentrated harder, feeling what it was like to be debt free. The trips to the mailbox continued to disappoint. Things were getting down to the wire, and I was beginning to lose hope.

One day in mid-March, I had a very early breakfast meeting for work at a local restaurant a few miles from the house. As I hustled out the door that morning, I expressed my love to David quickly and mindlessly. It was apparently just another normal day in our busy lives.

The meeting was inspiring and creative, leaving me feeling good about the work I was doing at the hospital. When it concluded, I walked briskly to the car, energized and ready to take on the world. As I often do, I grabbed my phone before starting the car to see what had transpired while I was in the meeting.

There was a voicemail from David.

"Christin, this is David. When you get this, please call me. Here's my number. . . Thank you."

Suddenly, it felt as if all of the oxygen had been sucked out of the car. Time stood still. The sound of my heart breaking pulsated in my ears.

Have you ever gotten that pit in your stomach when you know your whole world is about to change? Your skin crawls. You can't catch your breath. Your head spins. You suddenly start sweating. David called me during the workday, sounded so calm, *and* left me his cell phone number in the message (the same cell phone number he has had for twenty years). I couldn't breathe.

"Hey, babe! I just got out of my meeting and listened to your message. What's up?"

"Thank you for calling me back. This morning, I began the process of refinancing our mortgage. I pulled our credit reports. Are you aware it shows you have a balance of $33,000 on your American Express?"

This was exactly why I checked my phone *before* I start driving. These types of unexpected conversations almost never happen, but every once in a while, they do, and they would definitely cause an accident. I could hear my heartbeat consume the air in the car, like surround sound that I couldn't turn down. *Damn it.*

Inhale. Exhale. How do I answer this? Poor David doesn't deserve this. All he asked of me was not to create debt. Not only had I created debt, I'd created quite a bit of debt. I broke my promise.

"Yes."

My yes hung in the air like a lead balloon. I braced. Please, feel free to let me have it. I totally deserve it. How the heck did I get here?

"Okay. Thank you for telling me the truth and not making up something to try to deny it. This is what we're going to do from here on out. I'm now in charge of our finances. We'll work together to create a budget and a plan, but we'll no longer put our family at risk by doing this separately."

Did I hear that correctly? Did someone get that on tape? David just calmly replied to the discovery that I had totally screwed up again—in a *big* way—by sharing that we were going to combine our finances after eighteen years and integrate our vision.

I spent the rest of the day uneasy, waiting for the other shoe to drop. There was no way I was going to survive this discovery without some sort of war breaking out. I had screwed up royally; I hadn't kept my end of the bargain, so there was sure to be a fallout. As I drove home that afternoon, I became sad and anxious with anticipation.

David, my angel, never spoke another word of it again. He handed me a form to transfer my direct deposit to our joint account. He asked for a few passcodes here and there. A few weeks later, we started going over the family budget together and our credit card statements together. We became closer, stronger, and more aligned. We worked through misunderstandings and old perceptions. I actually shopped less because I had an accountability partner. As a united couple, we made purchase decisions together. Our retirement accounts grew, and our decisions to cook at home increased. Together, we made incredible financial decisions which bonded us at a deeper level.

This manifestation taught me many lessons, including how foundational honesty is. Once David and I decided to share our financial journey together, I was able to see the truth; I'd spent my entire life buying things to feed an underlying hunger that was insatiable. The consumption I exploited was not filling the deep internal void that permeated. It gave me the high I desired for a moment, but it never lasted long. The hunger I'd been trying to fill was actually within me—the connection to myself. It wasn't the outside things that were my true desire, it was me—knowing, loving, and connecting with myself.

I had officially manifested my vision. It definitely wasn't the way I thought it would happen, like receiving a random check in the mail. As uncomfortable as it was when it arrived, I actually manifested something way better. The debt was managed by March 31, but the true freedom it continued to provide was priceless: the honest, vulnerable truth I shared with my husband, the opportunity to sit in the discomfort of creating debt once again, and the discovery of *why* I found myself in that situation once more. What hole was I trying to fill? What did I think I could buy that would make me happy? For what was I searching so desperately? These deep-seated questions came to the surface during this experience, though it would take a few more years and experiences for me to fully understand and address them.

UNDER
THE TUSCAN SUN

———

JULY 2018

On our wellbeing journey, David and I were blessed to spend time with and learn from a number of pioneering leaders in health and wellness. As usual, David was the first one who dug deep and found inspiration from these incredible thought leaders. He started listening to a podcast hosted by an ultra-athlete, recovering attorney, plant-based pioneer, and super interesting and intelligent human named Rich Roll. Each week, you could hear *The Rich Roll Podcast* flowing out of our home speakers. I found myself mesmerized by Rich's depth, word choice, intuitive line of questioning, and diverse parade of guests. While his platform's themes were peace and plants, he was clearly also a deep soul whose unique back story provided a level of depth and reflection that engaged both David and I for different reasons.

Rich's impact on our health was foundational and permeated so many different aspects of our lives. When we found out he was going to be attending and speaking at Seed Food & Wine Fest in Miami, we marked our calendars, bought tickets, and anticipated the chance to be in the same vicinity as this man who was rocking our world.

In November 2016, we found ourselves enjoying an incredible party at Miami Beach's Fountain Blue Hotel as the Seed Festival was kicking off. It was a Burger Battle, and forty different chefs showcased their plant-based burgers to a crowd of hundreds. The joint was jumping, and my energy and excitement were at full throttle. I felt swanky on the outdoor lawn, surrounded by beautiful vegans, dressed up, and hob knobbing. This was not my typical Thursday night.

After roaming the party for about an hour, we spotted Rich Roll across the lawn. He was chatting with John Salley, the former NBA player who was also a plant-based superstar. They were in a roped off section of the party with a handful of other clearly special guests. David and I, in true groupie style, sauntered over by the rope and watched. There was little we wouldn't do to have a conversation with Rich, just to share with him how much he had impacted our lives.

After about twenty minutes of taking it all in, I felt too old to be this much of a stalker. We turned our attention to the inviting sound of the band and slowly migrated away from the rope to better experience the live music.

As we settled into our new scene, we noticed a very sensual, beautiful, and free-spirited woman with long, flowing chestnut-brown hair, gently moving her body to the soothing beat of the band. She stood out. She was larger than life. Her style, her aura, her centeredness, and her light were breathtaking. David and I soon realized we were taking in Julie Piatt, Rich Roll's wife. She wasn't behind the ropes; she was among the people, taking in the vibe. She was understated, yet totally not. She was welcoming, but not of this world. She was stunning, yet approachable. I had never encountered a woman like her before.

Of course, David had the courage to walk right up to her and casually began a conversation. He shared that we were fans of both her and Rich and that our lives had been deeply moved because of their work. We were blessed to spend several minutes conversing with her. We shared plant-based stories and dove into my work in health care. We were united in the importance of lifestyle and food for our overall wellbeing. To respect her celebrity and privacy, we expressed gratitude for the time shared with her, then watched her float off to rejoin her famous husband.

Throughout the weekend we continued to run into Julie at a number of additional events. We attended a talk that she and Rich gave at the main festival event. It was inspiring to see them in action, both as individuals and as a couple.

For the next year, we expanded our consumption of Rich and Julie by adding her podcast to our menu. She was incredibly spiritual in her offerings, which stirred something deep within me. While I could not yet put my finger on it, I was shifting and blossoming under the guidance of this powerful and mystically divine woman. The influence occurred at a subconscious level, yet I was aware enough to be grateful for it and continue to follow my intuition, spending time in this space.

November 2017 rolled around, and we headed back to Seed Miami for another weekend of delicious food and festivities. We were full of excitement to take in another amazing weekend celebrating plant-based eating, yet also hopeful to reconnect with Rich and Julie. We were thrilled this year to attend the festival with Scott and Jenny Kashman, who shared our love for delicious vegan food and, of course, Rich Roll. As luck would have it, Rich and Julie were indeed present at the Friday night dinner we selected to attend.

David and Scott weren't shy. As soon as it was time to sit down at the long community tables for dinner, the boys boldly marched over to the vacant seats next to Rich and asked if it was okay to sit down. Rich graciously invited the four of us to sit. I could barely contain myself. I get physically uncomfortable being a groupie, yet I was excited and impressed that the boys had pulled this off.

David enjoyed familiar dialogue with Julie and shared that we had met her last year at this festival.

"Julie, Christin and I really enjoyed meeting you last year and have been following your work over the past twelve months. It's great to see you again."

Julie smiled and responded, "Yes, I remember connecting with you both. You were passionate promoters of lifestyle medicine."

Given the number of people she must meet, I was impressed that she remembered specific details about us.

Again, my hubby showed off his knowledge of their work and asked how their summer retreat to Ireland had gone. Julie lit up at this question, as this was her pet project. She spent a few minutes telling us the highlights of the amazing experience she and Rich hosted.

"We had an incredible experience in Ireland, but we'll be heading back to Italy next summer. The oasis at which we host the retreat in the hills of Tuscany is simply magical. You guys should come next year."

There was no need to ask me twice. I totally wanted to go to Italy with Rich and Julie, as well as thirty-six other super lucky people. It wouldn't be an inexpensive outing, but it would be once in a lifetime. For the months that followed, I watched David research the trip and budget accordingly so we could head to this intriguing experience in July.

"Babe, this is so exciting. Do you really think we can pull this off? It's a lot of money. Clearly it would be epic, but are you sure we can do this?"

The response I repeatedly received from my husband surprised me, considering he was an incredibly conservative banker.

"Honey, you need to go on this trip. We'll make it happen for you. Julie is going to help you heal and you're going to learn so much. This trip will change your life."

He was right. After all the years I'd been with David, he knew the struggles I continually had with my health. No one tried harder than I did to figure it out, and we were both realizing that maybe the answers to my health problems were not something that we'd find the traditional way.

This did sound a little dramatic to me, however. I felt I was doing exceptionally well, all things considered, and didn't require any *healing,* per say. Still, I'd definitely take a trip to Italy any time. We made our plans, bought our flights and travel insurance, and began counting down the days to our upcoming summer excursion with our favorite plant-based celebrity and his spiritual guide wife.

In mid-July 2018, we set off for Tuscany. I had decided that I would spend all ten days disconnected from any and all electronic devices. The world would survive without me plugging in, and I knew it would fuel my soul to rest from the outside noise. I would work on my presence. It took the first two days in Florence to adapt to not checking my phone every few minutes, yet I quickly began to feel light and free from being disconnected.

David and I soaked in the incredible culture and vibe of Florence for a few days. Soon, it was time to head off into the countryside to begin the retreat. As we approached the estate, we immediately felt at peace, noticing the isolated location and elegant simplicity of the property. There were vines for days and a few rustic and beautiful brick dwellings. Noticeably absent were any signs of commercialism, which we also found refreshing. As usual, David was right. This was exactly what my soul needed. We reached our room, unpacked our sparse belongings, and settled into our new home. In the background, we could hear the pleasant sounds of new acquaintances making friendly introductions and connecting for the first time. We decided to join in, and headed to the main gathering building. This would be the primary location where we would spend the next seven days, connecting with ourselves and new friends.

I was brimming with anticipation for a week of yoga, meditation, delicious plant-based meals, hikes, cooking demonstrations, and other wonderful surprises. It was easy to settle in and let my guard down. I was open to receive whatever divine treats Julie and Rich had in store for us. I couldn't help but giggle. Many of the attendees were on this journey because of the celebrity status of Rich. Getting to spend a week in Tuscany with him was indeed mind-blowing, but David and I were acutely aware of Julie's magic. While perhaps the less *famous* side of the couple, she was definitely foundational and powerful. It didn't take long to experience this. Her presence and power were breathtaking, filling any room she entered.

The following morning, we rose early, eager to begin our first full day. We spent the first two hours enjoying jai yoga and meditating. My body and soul stretched beyond my dreams and opened up my capacity to explore and receive.

The group prepared to transition to our next activity. We grabbed chairs from the storage closet and settled in to witness the dynamic couple's first presentation. Julie spoke first.

"We're going to spend time this week healing from past wounds. On Tuesday, each of you will enjoy some alone time out in nature and contemplate your inaugural triggering event."

Wait, what? Seriously, you're going to make me waste time on grave digging up the past?

I was *over* my original triggering event. Been there, done that. I had spent lots of money on therapy. There was no need to revisit it. It doesn't define me. I came on this retreat to walk toward enlightenment, not dwell on the past. This was not what I signed up for.

Julie shared that further instruction would be coming, but for now, she was just sharing a high-level overview of our week. I tried to let it go, but I was still very disturbed that this exercise was on the schedule because I had already done heaps of work on this kind of stuff. Perhaps I would come up with a better way to spend a few hours in Tuscany on my own accord.

As promised, on Tuesday I found myself receiving further instructions for the afternoon exercise. We were to revisit our original triggering event.

"We all have experiences that have hurt us. Today, we're going to find a spot on this beautiful property and sit alone in nature. Please bring a notepad, some drawing pencils, and something to write with."

We came to Tuscany to grow into the future, not obsess about the past. I had already done so much work. I felt complete. I worked with a therapist as a late teen, young adult, in both of my marriages, with Carolyn in hypnotherapy, and with countless others. Still displeased with the idea of wasting time on this exercise, I worked to open myself up to it. I scanned the other attendees to see how they were reacting, but no one else seemed overly bothered. Perhaps I was alone in my displeasure. I focused back in on Julie delivering the instructions.

"When you settle into your corner of nature, close your eyes and take yourself back to that original event. Sit with it. Experience all of its pain and discomfort. I want you to *feel* it. See it. Smell it. Hear it. Take it all in. Don't turn away from it. Instead, let it all wash over you. Truly relive the experience."

This seemed simple enough. Once we had fully relived it, we were to open our eyes and journal the experience and write out each and every detail we could remember. That would complete the first part of the exercise. Julie began explaining the next section.

"Next, take your time and rewrite the story. How would you change it if you could? What would you do differently? What would an alternate outcome look like? Let this rewriting pour out of you."

The third and final part of this exercise would be to draw a picture of this new experience, expressing how it made us feel and what it meant to us. On Thursday evening, we'd participate in a burning ceremony where we would lay this event to rest.

I begrudgingly left the room to collect my items as instructed. For good measure, I added a roll of toilet paper, as I knew this was going to produce a vast number of tears. After kissing David goodbye, I roamed among the vineyards to find my landing spot. I came across a shady green patch of grass under a beautiful tree that felt right. As I sat, I appreciated the expansive view overlooking row after row of vines. I took in a deep breath and began the journey back to a place I had no desire to revisit.

It was almost impossible, at first, to truly allow myself to revisit this time. Instead of shutting down the moment as it became real and terrifying, I supported myself in staying there. Letting it happen all over again made my heart race and body ache. I smelled it. I tasted it. I heard it. I saw it. I felt myself as that young girl, paralyzed with fear and devastation, unable to move away from the trauma and abuse. My heart ached for her and I wanted to snatch her and run far, far away. Instead, she and I relived each and every gory detail, using all of our senses.

As the revisit concluded, I came out of my trance. I expected to see half the roll of toilet paper used and soaking wet. Yet there it sat beside me, fully intact. *That was weird. I didn't shed a single tear. Did I do something wrong? How did I not cry?*

After giving myself a few minutes to regroup, I moved on to part two of this awful exercise. I began to write out the experience, journaling all of my sensory intake. I would smell the coffee on his breath and hear the seagulls outside. The sound of my heart pounding rapidly in my chest began to deafen me. I so desperately didn't want to have this happen again, yet I had nowhere to run. The words tumbled out onto the page, exposing every gruesome detail. The shame and sadness devoured my soul, but I willed myself to get it all out.

When there were no more words to express, I set the pen down and exhaled a long, deep sigh. I was surprised that I didn't shed a single tear. *What should I make of that? What's wrong with me? This is the saddest thing I've ever experienced. I'm whole heartedly feeling all of my emotions, yet I'm not crying my eyeballs out.*

Now, it was time to rewrite the story that had haunted my entire existence. One I swore I had already healed from. It occurred to me that I hadn't actually healed from it; I had emphatically and quite profoundly managed it, stuffed it, ignored it, and denied it. I hadn't let it truly run through me, exhale it, and let it go. I hadn't healed.

So, how would this new story unfold? What would have been a much better journey that would've spared me the emotional, mental, and physical abuse that I survived? I wouldn't wish it on my worst enemy. Fortunately, there in Tuscany, I had the chance to rewrite history.

As I sat, appreciating the Tuscan sun under a big, inviting cypress tree, armed with my roll of toilet paper and journal, the answer intuitively and clearly revealed itself. I grew into the woman I had become *because* of my hardships. Because I overcame them. Because I worked tirelessly to support others who experienced them. Because I forgave them. Apparently, the only person I hadn't given permission to heal from this trauma was myself. Perhaps this would be the day. In that moment I was 100 percent sure there was nothing to change. My experiences were forever a part of me—a badge of survival, courage, and resilience.

Instead, I wrote a letter to my parents, my brother, my husband, my incredible step kids, my cousin, my bestie, my first husband, and to Scott. I thanked each and every one of them for the part they played in my life and expressed gratitude for the support and lessons along the way. I had grown from knowing each of them, and I wouldn't change one darned thing about my life. While it was a bit crazy, it was mine, and I whole heartedly loved and embraced each and every turn in the road.

At the beginning of the retreat, I hadn't seen any of this coming. David saw what I hadn't all along, so he worked diligently to provide this incredible healing opportunity for me. A few days ago, I was pissed I had to waste time revisiting something so old and buried. I thought it was a complete waste of time. Instead, after this exercise, I had experienced true trauma healing, holistically feeling peace and calm envelop me. I was safe. I was love. I was perfect, flawed and all. And I wouldn't change a darned thing.

RECEIVING

JULY 2018

Our Tuscany retreat with Rich and Julie included a session with either an acupuncturist or an Ayurvedic practitioner. Prior to departing for Italy, I read the information on both offerings and decided acupuncture seemed like the best fit for me and David. I booked the sessions for us and didn't put much thought into it afterwards.

As the week of the retreat unfolded, attendees would peel off and partake in their one-on-one appointment for the treatment they'd chosen. The practitioners, Colin and Jennifer, both interacted with us during mealtime. It was an absolute pleasure getting to know both of them as individuals. My acupuncture experience with Colin was impactful and furthered my healing process. Yet, my casual connection with Jennifer during mealtimes and watching her interact with attendees in her downtime left me feeling like I needed to connect with her.

I was unfamiliar with Ayurvedic medicine and didn't understand how it worked or its origins. Throughout the week, I witnessed Jennifer sitting quietly with guests. She would place her fingers on their wrist and it seemed as if she was reading something. It was like she was taking their blood pressure. The information she would share after seemed to move folks deeply. I wanted her to hold my wrist, too! As the week continued to fly by, I worked up the courage to approach her and ask if she would spend a few minutes with me. The day before our retreat concluded, I finally asked her. She gladly made time to connect with me.

She offered me about five minutes for a quick assessment. We sat quietly after lunch, huddled in the corner of the dining area. She placed her two fingers on my wrist. I sat still, excited to learn what she would discover. Many other attendees had shared how transformative her reading was, and I was ready to hear mine.

We sat with our eyes closed, taking deep, relaxing breaths. After about ninety seconds of quiet, I felt her jolt. When I opened my eyes, I found Jennifer had also opened hers, wide. Compassionate, deep concern emanated from her. She took a deep breath, and began to speak evenly and kindly.

"I have no idea how you're sitting here right now."

Interesting. Not sure what she means by that. I've been here all week, enjoying and growing. What does she mean?

She continued.

"You're totally depleted. You have no fuel, no energy, nothing left to give. You've been giving and giving all of yourself for so long. At the same time, you're deflecting any receiving. You'll not allow yourself to receive from others, and you won't give to yourself. You should be in an emergency room right now. You're dangerously close to a medically emergent breakdown."

Needless to say, this wasn't what I was expecting. I thought I would learn about what types of food were best for me to consume, or something like what the other guests were raving about. Instead, I heard that I was completely void of fuel, the result of living a life that was only flowing in one direction.

I sat with the information for a moment and tried to let it sink in. I was at a loss for words, unsure of how to interpret her words.

The announcement that our next group session would be starting momentarily jostled me out of my reflection. I thanked Jennifer and, in a daze, walked toward the collective for our next experience.

I never had the pleasure of connecting with Jennifer again. I'd simply received the information I was destined to receive from her divine work. As I unpacked her message over the next few days, I realized she was absolutely spot on. In a few brief moments, I received the help, inspiration, and intervention I needed from her words. I *was* exhausted; I was tired of faking my positivity and joy at work or in support of others when I felt so depleted all the time. I constantly willed myself to rally and serve. At the same time, I didn't welcome others into my heart. I disdained the discomfort of receiving and deflected it professionally and gracefully without the other person ever knowing the difference. No one could get inside. I was a steel trap, welded shut and deeply entrenched, never accessed, hurt, or affected. I was safe deep down in there; if no one could touch me, no one could truly hurt me. I gave all of me and received nothing.

By now, it was coming into focus that these issues were linked to my childhood trauma; I was keeping people and experiences at a distance so I'd be safe and not get hurt. At that moment, I knew my behavior wasn't sustainable. I was weak and exhausted.

This realization made me severely sad, deep in my soul, especially because it had caused me to teeter on the brink of a medical breakdown. My newfound awareness motivated me to explore how to open myself up to receiving and how to go about refueling myself.

INSPIRE AWAKENING

FALL 2018

As part of my work at the hospital, I ran our wellness centers. It felt ironic to me that they didn't operate as wellness centers at all; they were gyms. When I took over, there was so much opportunity to create a center where people could convene to be well, so I set out to create just that.

We established educational opportunities for the community that would support their wellbeing journey. We created a dedicated "Mind & Body" program, offering multiple yoga and meditation programs daily. We offered a lending library, enhanced our healthy food offerings, and brought in a nutritionist a few days a week to round out the experience. You could even purchase essential oils.

My favorite additions occurred in the treatment rooms. Once a space only occasionally used for massages, we added acupuncture, reiki, craniosacral therapy, an amethyst mat, and Carolyn, the hypnotherapist. The community couldn't believe it—a hospital, hosting these alternative modalities!

Folks were excited and drove from miles away to use these wonderful resources. My excitement grew as we transformed from a gym to an actual wellness center.

Twice a week, Carolyn drove over an hour to see clients at the center. I rarely ever saw her, as I was busy, and she was booked. One day I bumped into her in the ladies' locker room, excited to reconnect and hear how her sessions were going.

"I'm loving it here! Thanks for having me. It's inspiring to help people reflect and heal while enhancing and improving the work they're doing on themselves in other ways. This is really great."

I was so proud and thankful for her gifts and commitment. Carolyn was such a special person to me both personally and professionally. The work I'd done with her had truly been a vital part of my healing.

"Thank you, Carolyn. I'm so grateful you're here and for the work that you do."

"My pleasure, but when are *you* going to come see me? I see you're working like crazy. Are you taking time for self-care?"

I smiled. She was so silly. I was the System Director of Health and Wellness. What work did I need to do on myself? All was well. I had already done this work and was good. I appreciated the thoughtfulness but dismissed the idea.

"I'm all set, Carolyn, but thank you! No more work to be done here. Thanks, though."

A knowing smile crept up on her angelic face.

"I insist. We need to reconnect. I wrap up with clients at 4:00 p.m. Let's sit for a bit and catch up."

A few hours later, I found myself in her treatment room. We chitchatted for a bit, and I was amused that she thought I still needed help.

"I'd love to do a session with you to explore your purpose. Do you know what your purpose is? I know it's on our Wellness Wheel, but I would love to learn more about yours, specifically."

Well, of course I knew that purpose was on our Wellness Wheel; I was the one who came up with the idea!

Of course I know what my purpose is. It's to. . .

It's to what? Hmm, that's interesting. What is my purpose? Clearly it's to help people, but help people what? Get healthy? Work out? Eat right?

"Thanks, Carolyn. I appreciate your kind inquiry. I'm very much living a life of purpose. I help people. I'm very fulfilled. You're always looking out for me, and I appreciate you."

Carolyn wouldn't accept this answer. Clearly, she thought my purpose was vague at best. Exploring and fine-tuning one's purpose was one of her offerings, and it was time for me to sit down and do this work.

We spent the next few hours working to articulate my purpose. It was incredible that I was having such a difficult time putting it into words. Nothing felt right. I lived my purpose daily but didn't know how to express it.

I help people be well.

I support others on their wellness journey.

I'm here to enhance wellbeing.

Nothing felt right.

After what seemed to be an eternity, I heard myself say,

"I inspire awakening."

Boom. The words hung in the air. The silence was deafening. I looked at Carolyn as it settled in and visibly saw her shoulders relax. While I had never birthed a child, I felt like I had just delivered triplets.

I inspire awakening.

"That's it, Carolyn. That's my purpose. I inspire awakening. Wow, what a feeling! I feel calm, surreal, whole, and full. I inspire awakening."

Carolyn also looked a little worn out from this experience. She smiled, clearly thrilled that we had uncovered my deep-seated purpose.

"I can't thank you enough for taking the time to walk through this with me, Carolyn. Your work is so impactful. I didn't realize I had more work to do, but clearly identifying my purpose was no doubt a missing piece of the puzzle. I'll be forever grateful that you insisted that we pause and do this work."

We said our goodbyes and went our separate ways. *I inspire awakening.* The words calmed me and spoke to my soul. I knew it was right the second it came out of my mouth. Despite how comfortable and comforting it felt to say them out loud, their irony was not lost on me.

I had no idea what they meant.

What does it mean to inspire awakening? Awaken what? And who do I think I am that I can inspire someone? How arrogant?

Feeling like I had found the right words clashed with the total uncertainty of what the words actually meant. I had found my purpose statement, my reason for being. There was no doubt in my mind about that. I just had no idea what it meant. I would spend the next few years growing into the understanding of my purpose in life, as well as sitting in the discomfort of the uncertainty.

LIGHTHOUSE

———

NOVEMBER 2018

Late fall was in full bloom, and our subtropical oasis was buzzing with seasonal activity. Calendars brimmed with a multitude of ways to recreate and experience all of the diverse offerings southwest Florida hosted each year for our residents and guests alike.

As part of my work within the hospital system, I created a national speaker series which brought top thought leaders to our region. This series had grown into quite the community outreach; what had started as a small, niche group of followers who were open to learning more about lifestyle medicine grew to over one thousand attendees per speaker. Our reputation around the nation as a hotbed for plant-based living and preventative health blossomed. We were attracting the best of the best from around the globe, hosting leaders such as Dr. Darren Morton, Dr. Caldwell Esselstyn, Dr. T. Colin Campbell, Dr. Michael Gregor, Dr. David Katz, Dr. Garth Davis, and Dr. Neal Barnard. You probably can see where this is heading; they were all male doctors.

I wanted to diversify our speakers, and Julie Piatt would definitely fit the bill. She was a spiritual healer, a true north in helping me find my way to my higher self. She'd helped me heal, let go, and get in touch with the Universe. Our community was open to alternative healing, but I knew that with Julie, we'd be walking a thin line. It was possible that some audience members wouldn't embrace some of her views and opinions. My desire was to provide new ways of thinking while being respectful to the health care system which provided this offering. A presentation from Julie had the potential to touch those who were open and ready to explore healing in a whole new way. Perhaps the traditional way of trying to be healthy had failed them, just as it had failed me.

As the event approached, my excitement grew. We were hosting Julie's community talk on national election night of all nights, but that was how the schedule had worked out. I knew this fact would reduce our attendance, but I was comfortable with that since this presentation was going to be more spiritual and alternative than the ones our previous doctors had given. Julie's extensive experience with yoga, meditation, ritual, spirituality, and alignment with the subconscious mind would be a truly different approach.

Julie would be flying into Miami, so David suggested we drive the two and a half hours to the airport to pick her up. It only seemed fitting, since it would have been inconsiderate to ask her to Uber. She was our distinguished guest, and selfishly, I was breathless at the idea of having the long return trip to pick her brain and simply be in her energy field.

Late that Sunday afternoon, we drove Alligator Alley toward Miami International Airport. David and I were both animated with anticipation, like two middle schoolers talking over each other with palatable excitement. Julie and her husband had made quite an impact on our lives, and now she was going to be in our hometown as our guest!

The airport, as always, was chaotic and overflowing; people from all over the world enter and exit this vibrant city that offers a delicious blend of diversity and culture. We parked and made our way inside, and my heart rate elevated as I took in the tempo. Cars honked, languages foreign to my ear floated in the air, and so many different kinds of people walked past us. You could cut the energy with a knife. We made it to baggage claim to await Julie's arrival, excited and very nervous about hosting such a distinguished, powerful guest.

Suddenly, there she was. She floated down the escalator with her aura that expanded for miles around. I watched Julie approach us as if she was walking on air. She stood so tall and regal, with her long hair flowing and a fabulous statement hat perched high on her uplifted head. She composed herself with an ease and grace that was both sensual and strong. I felt like all air in the terminal was rushing toward her and the stir she left behind her moved molecules. She radiated, and I couldn't believe I was going to spend the next forty-eight hours hosting her.

We drove back to Fort Myers in the dark of the night, and I soaked in the opportunity to spend the car ride listening to her wisdom, experiences, and vision. She was by far the most deeply in-tune spiritual person I had ever met, and with each sentence she spoke, I listened acutely and absorbed with great thirst.

I was still reeling from attending her life-altering retreat in Tuscany she hosted with her husband, Rich Roll. That trip had deeply impacted me, providing a level of understanding and healing that became the catalyst for my true growth and health. Yet, this intimate experience driving in our car would be the connection that would provide me with the courage and desire to grow in my own spiritual practice. I was giddy with excitement, hoping the event attendees would get a taste of this awareness—that optimal wellbeing was not about taking medicine and repairing problems, but instead about healing our wounds and loving ourselves so that we could thrive.

The following day we left Julie to attend to her work and preparation while David and I carried on with our usual activities. As we were enjoying breakfast together, David asked what my plans were for the evening event.

"How are you going to format this evening's presentation?"

I was unsure what he meant by this question. We formatted the events the same way each time.

"What do you mean, honey? I'm going to introduce Julie, then Julie will present, then we will offer the audience a Q&A."

"Are you sure you want to do that? Julie's lens is going to be quite different than those of the previous speakers you've hosted. Plus, this is a hospital event. You might want to consider sitting on stage with her and doing it more as an interview. This way, if things go too deep into alternative health, you can redirect the conversation."

As was often the case, my husband was so right. I couldn't imagine life without him, nor trying to lead this pioneering work without his input. He helped bridge the gap between disruption and adaptation. Sometimes his answer was simple, but I was so entrenched that I'd missed it.

"Thank you, baby! That's an excellent idea. I'll put two chairs on the stage and host Julie interview-style."

Julie welcomed that idea, and we prepared a few questions for me to ask her. This way she would still have free rein to shine brightly but also provide a safety net if we started getting too outside of the box. This format also kept me more involved, which I loved. I would guide the conversation and shed light on takeaways that were impactful to me. It was a win-win.

All of a sudden, it was showtime. As I stood on stage and introduced Julie, I was deeply and whole heartedly moved. It was surreal, and I allowed my heart to be open and feel how special this gathering truly was. Julie's message was about to touch hundreds of community members, an experience that was truly transformational for me just a few months earlier in the hills of Tuscany. I took a pause and looked at the folks seated in the front row. My heart was full of joy as I saw my husband, my stepdaughter, my best friend, and Scott and Jenny Kashman. As my eyes scanned the next few rows, I felt a continuation of joy and gratitude for being able to share this journey with so many wonderful, beautiful souls. This would be a very special night.

Julie arrived on stage much as she had at Miami International Airport; her vibrancy took up the entire auditorium and her presence and aura enveloped us all. You could hear a pin drop in this vast space, as all attention was dialed in to hear Julie's message. Our conversation flowed effortlessly as time flew by. Julie had such charisma and grace that the audience was hanging on her every word. I sat back in my chair with ease, taking it all in.

"So, Julie," I asked. "What would you say are some health benefits to yoga, ritual, and meditation?"

With incredible articulation, grace, and clarity, Julie shared how vital and foundational the mind-body connection was and the effects that being disconnected have on the physical form.

As time was beginning to close out, I began formatting the dialogue to bring things to a close. With the final question posed, Julie started sharing a story about her father and her husband. I knew Julie planned on sharing how much the passing of her father had affected her journey, but I had no idea how much it was about to affect mine.

Julie shared about her father's end of life. She chose to spend time by his side, caring for him and supporting his transition.

"I sat by his bedside in the quiet and held his hand. I spoke softly to him, read to him, and meditated with him."

That was a very special time, full of love and celebration. The shared rituals and dialogue that occurred between them provided a transformational way of dealing with the death of a loved one, a simplicity and beauty that deeply moved the audience.

As I absorbed her story, I heard her share a lesson she learned from her father during this transition. He expressed to her that life was about owning your own vision and journey and not imposing it upon others. We're each here to live our own lives, and it's not our role to project our experience as the truth for all.

I felt and heard her story. It rolled through my body, creating a warm sensation that deeply moved me. I listened, nodded, and smiled. What a beautiful message and a great way to wrap up the evening's program. As I prepared to make my final closing remarks and open things up for audience questions, she began speaking again.

She described a conversation she'd had with her husband Rich, and how she called him to extend an apology.

An apology? Wait, why was Julie calling Rich to apologize? What did she do wrong? Why did her father's sentiments spark this call? What did I miss?

Julie went on to explain that for the previous seven years, she'd been pressuring Rich to make lifestyle changes—to eat better, and embrace a more spiritual practice. Basically, she wanted him to follow the same growth pattern she did. Rich resisted, but Julie kept pushing. She could see so much untapped potential in him and wanted so badly for him to emerge into his higher purpose and light. During this call, she apologized for trying to impose her vision onto him. She released her judgement, asked for forgiveness, and expressed her deep love for him.

As I sat on the stage next to her, soaking in this story, my mind started to expand. I contemplated the countless number of times I assumed that my way of life was the most brilliant and only way to go. I wondered how many people onto whom I had imposed my beliefs, trying to control their paths.

How many phone calls did I have to make?

As my thoughts came back into the room, I realized she was sharing additional closure to her story. This takeaway was even more impactful.

A week after she had placed the phone call and asked Rich for forgiveness, he reached out to her.

"Hey, honey, can you give me the information for the juice cleanse you'd been telling me about? I think I'm going to give it a try."

Wait, what had just happened? Julie had been badgering Rich for seven years to try eating clean, cleanse, move, and meditate, and a week after she stopped pressuring him, he asked her for guidance? You can't make this stuff up! One person starting a juice cleanse might not seem like a big deal, but we have to put this into context; Rich Roll has gone on to be one of the most famous ultra-athletes on the planet who had completed five ultra-marathons on the five Hawaiian Islands in five days. He had transformed himself, and in turn, inspired transformation in hundreds of thousands of others. Ironically, this chapter for Rich began a week after Julie let go of trying to force it.

I absorbed this reality and I felt transported from the stage. I was lightheaded and frozen in time. Since birth, I had been telling people what to do and would always be upset if they didn't do things my way. I bossed around the neighborhood kids in my backyard sandbox growing up. I told my fellow teammates where to stand and how to throw. I projected onto my brother, my mother, my husband, my daughter, and my co-workers. I'd spent my entire life thinking I had all of the answers and that everyone should follow what I had to say.

Working so hard to convince others to move in my direction combined with needing to control my environment created a lifetime of acute stress that ran my autoimmune system into overdrive. An underlying chronic surge of fear and frustration threaded through my health history, creating many digestive issues, cancer, skin issues, and exhaustion.

Julie had just said that I'm only responsible for one human: myself. I don't need to—actually, I don't have the right to—project my vision onto others. My only role and responsibility were to know *me*, like *me*, and shine like a lighthouse. Now it all made sense. Be you. Like you. Shine on. Don't worry about anyone else. If others follow, great. If not, great. But know who you are and like that person.

As we concluded, a quiet calmness enveloped the audience. Most attendees remained in their seats as Julie and I made our way to the front entrance of the auditorium to prepare for her book signing. While we walked past the sea of community friends and supporters, I could feel their contemplation in the air. People were having some literal breakthroughs and reflecting on many things Julie had said. Yet, the most profound part of the evening was the seed planting that had occurred. The deeply-rooted impact of Julie's words had fertilized a shift for audience members on which they couldn't yet put their finger, but their plants would blossom over the months and years to come.

PART 4

LETTING GO
AND AWAKENING
WITH PURPOSE

SAYING YES TO
THE UNIVERSE

———

APRIL 2019

It was a typical evening in southwest Florida, one where many community leaders came together to honor the work of the incredible individuals and organizations who continuously supported the development and growth of our region. We were gathered at the Hyatt Regency Coconut Point this particular evening to celebrate our dear friends, Scott and Diana Willis and Dave Copham, as they joined the esteemed group of laureates for Junior Achievement. The ballroom was bustling with excitement as vibrant community leaders flitted about hugging one another, creating bonds, and making small talk.

There was something else in the air this particular evening; news had recently broken that one of the five County Commissioners for our area was very ill and would pass away shortly. This was very upsetting news, and folks were abuzz discussing who should be appointed to take his place if and when this would occur. Lee County's Board of County Commission was comprised of five white males. No judgment to any of them, but 53 percent of Lee County was made up of women. Yet, there was no diversity in this governing board. A number of prominent leaders—particularly women—were on a mission to have the Governor rectify this situation by appointing a woman. So, the hunt was on to find the right woman who had the aptitude, talent, and tough skin to take on the job.

Many women in the crowd that night were prospective candidates. A few expressed interest and put their name on this list. Toward the end of the evening, a very vibrant, strong leader happened upon our event table and warmly smiled. She asked how I was doing and if I'd heard the news about Commissioner Kiker's rapidly declining health. She then asked me if I would be interested in being appointed to the post.

I paused, breathed in her words, and let them sink in. While many in the past had inquired if I would be open to running for public office, it had truly never spoken to me. But, in this current moment, I was at a crossroads at work and was practicing the art of saying yes to the universe even when things didn't seem to make a whole lot of sense. I heard myself say to her,

"Thank you, I'm honored that you feel I would be a good fit. I'd be happy to learn more about the appointment."

She covered her surprise well and replied,

"Really? Wow. That's great news! You'd make a wonderful Commissioner. I'll give you a call this week and we can discuss things further."

And off she went.

I honestly didn't think much about it. I actually figured she'd never call. There was a lot of buzz about the potential opening and lots of female candidates, so I assumed it wouldn't go anywhere. I was truly humbled that she asked, but I didn't even mention it to my husband on the way home since nothing would come from it.

A few days later, my phone rang. Surprisingly, it was the amazing, vivacious community leader checking in to see if I would be open to a discussion with some political legends to further explore the idea of County Commission. I once again heard myself agree to further exploration, and we set up a lunch meeting for the following week.

I hung up the phone and contemplated that word might get out. It was time to bring this to my husband for further internal review.

"Honey, I've been asked if I would be interested in serving our community as County Commissioner if Commissioner Kiker passes away. I shared that I'd be open to learning more and have been asked to have lunch next week to discuss further. What are your thoughts?"

I so love my husband. Literally, since the day I met him, he has been supportive and open to my unconventional thoughts and decisions, even when they make him uncomfortable, or they went against popular opinion.

"You'd be an amazing Commissioner, but why would you ever want to do it? Politics are ugly. People spread lies about you and exploit untruths. It would be a ton of thankless work. Why would you say yes?"

My answer was simple.

"Because I can."

I realized that I was in a unique position. I knew a lot of people in our area based on the work I'd done over the past decade. I knew my style of leadership was one of bringing people together and finding common ground. In its current state, regional politics were very, very polarized. I had the experience and skillset to find solutions to which we could all agree. I also knew my skin was thick enough; what others may say about me might hurt, but it wouldn't throw me off-course and take me places I didn't want to go. I also knew that I had a husband who could handle the public exposure. We'd been living an open-book journey for quite some time and understood the responsibility and inconsistencies that came from living this way.

We needed a woman in leadership. We needed collaboration, authenticity, and transparency. We needed the female spirit represented and I was uniquely qualified to do the job. I had a responsibility to at least be open to the role, and—who was I kidding—I'd never get it anyway.

Commissioner Kiker passed away. The community honored his life and work. We said goodbye and consoled his wife. The need to appoint a replacement was of vital importance and would be the Governor's first political appointment. Many candidates jockeyed for this position, including deeply-rooted political players with high aspirations for public service. And yes, most of them were white men.

In the meantime, I attended the exploratory lunch. I then connected with other strong supporters and filled out the application for this role. Many I spoke with thought I was crazy but were thrilled I was considering taking this on. They graciously offered their support. My hospital CEO fully supported my application and was willing to work with my schedule if I was indeed selected. We were off to a surreal start.

A few weeks in, I received a call from a very powerful political supporter who asked if I would be open to chatting with a former state senator who remained very active in the political arena. He now owned a large real estate development company and was extremely interested in who might be appointed. To be clear, he was openly supporting another potential appointee, but I was happy to connect with him and answer any questions he may have. I had nothing to hide and welcomed the opportunity to share whatever information he was interested in.

A few hours later, I took this call. Right out of the gate, the uncomfortable questions started.

"So, are you pro-life or pro-choice?"

Here we go. Southwest Florida was a *very* conservative part of the country and I knew this subject would upset a number of people.

I replied, "County Commission doesn't sit in the seat to legislate on this issue."

Of course, he couldn't leave the topic alone, but I didn't care if he did or not. I was very comfortable with who I was and where I stood on this issue.

"Well, while County Commission might not make these decisions, the Governor and the Republican Party are very pro-life. You need to be, too."

I thanked him for his guidance and shared that I was aware that the Governor and the local Republican leadership were pro-life. Then I shared my history.

"I can't imagine being in the position to have to consider aborting a pregnancy. It must be an incredibly heart-wrenching, life-altering decision to have to make. I choose not to sit in judgment of women who are faced with this decision. My heart and love go out to them. I support preventing pregnancy, sexual abuse, and rape. I encourage education and open dialogue so that no woman has to be faced with such a decision."

I continued.

"And, since we're on the subject, I'll also share that I'm a strong supporter of Planned Parenthood. When I was twenty-one years old and a recent college graduate, I found myself uninsured and potentially getting involved in a relationship. I needed birth control and sought out their services. During my appointment, a doctor discovered that I had ovarian cancer, and they saved my life. As a result, I've never had the pleasure of being pregnant and birthing children, but thanks to their health care services, I'm still here today."

I had to admit, that felt good. I assumed this would put the issue to bed. What was anyone going to say to that? Surprisingly, I heard something much different.

"Well, you need to pray on that. Just lie. Say you're pro-life or else your political career will never work out."

There were few moments in life when I found myself speechless. This was one of those times. It truly took me a few seconds to recover. Here was a guy who presented himself as a conservative, religious leader, yet his advice to me was to pray on it and then lie. Mind you, when he represented us in Tallahassee decades before, he was a Democrat. Now, he showcased himself as an über-conservative. Maybe my husband was right. Why would I ever want to expose myself to people like this?

Our conversation went on for quite some time. I'd never been interrogated before, but after our call, I had a really strong idea of what it must feel like. Despite his grilling, I kept myself centered, honest, transparent, and true to my values. I shared any and all experiences that he might perceive as skeletons so that they were out in the open, including my $500 contribution to Democratic Commission of Agriculture candidate Nikki Fried. When he asked why I would donate to a Democrat, I shared that Nikki Fried was pro agriculture and impactful economic development, as was I. I emphasized that working across political parties would be essential to finding common ground and creating forward movement. Instead of him admiring and celebrating this about me, he suggested it was shameful and must be stopped.

I worked to end our discussion. I expressed gratitude for the opportunity to connect and offered to be available in the future if I could be of service or if he had any additional questions. As we closed, he asked me several more things.

"Why do you want this position? What are your political aspirations? What are you trying to accomplish?"

The answers were simple.

"I've been asked to serve in this capacity. If the Governor would like me to, I'm happy to do so. If he doesn't, then I won't. That sums it up. I sit in the unique position to serve in this capacity and am willing to do so. This isn't about *me*."

And with that, I hung up the phone.

UNATTACHED
TO OUTCOME

———

MAY 2019

My life was full of incredibly vibrant and successful friends
with whom I was blessed to walk life and learned so much
from. Heather Christie was one of those friends.

Heather was a nationally celebrated thought leader, public
speaker, and executive coach. I had admired her for years,
and I watched her rocket speed trajectory in both her per-
sonal and professional growth. Heather was very intentional
in her support of my development and growth, also. She
made time to attend events I chaired and the speeches I gave.
She donated, gave feedback, and spoke words of inspiration
and encouragement.

Heather was also the first person to tell me that I was off
the charts in the "I" section of the DiSC assessment. The
"I" stood for "influencer," one motivated by social recogni-
tion, group activities, and relationships. We prioritize taking

action, collaboration, and expressing enthusiasm, and are often described as warm, trusting, optimistic, magnetic, enthusiastic, and convincing. Learning this about myself was a huge step in helping me understand how I was wired. So, while I couldn't spend a ton of time with Heather due to our busy schedules, she was such an important part of my awakening.

That day in May of 2019, I felt grateful that we'd set aside some time to get together and feed our souls. Inevitably, when I spent time with her, I always left with a lesson that would rock me to my core. This day would be no exception.

It was a Wednesday. I had settled in my car for the more than two-hour drive to Miami. I was finishing up an incredible year-long experience with Leadership Florida and was crossing the state for our final multi-day gathering as a cohort. The wisdom, knowledge, and relationships I acquired in this program over the past twelve months exceeded my expectations. I was excited to reconnect with my class and put the finishing touches on this incredible experience.

Heather and I had set up a time to chat during this long car ride across Alligator Alley. Accessing my Bluetooth, I excitedly gave her a call. As usual, we fired off rapid questions to one another, hungry to catch up on the latest and greatest happenings in each other's worlds. We both laughed as we accidentally talked over each other in our excitement. She took command and asserted,

"Wait, you go first. I'm dying to know what's going on with this political appointment you've applied for! It's so incredible! Are you excited? What made you decide to apply for it?"

My energy immediately lowered. I exhaled and replied,

"I'm not excited about it. I never saw myself in politics, but someone asked if I would serve. So, I agreed to open myself up to it. You know how I roll. Say *yes* to the Universe! And, if it's meant to be, it will be. Often, I don't understand why some things cross my path, but I've learned to just go with the flow and see what unfolds."

Heather, my forever guide and brilliant coach, replied back.

"No, I get it. It's wonderful when we open ourselves up to unforeseen opportunities that aren't on our radar and we explore what they may bring! On a scale of one to ten, how excited are you about the opportunity?"

Without having to think too hard about my response, I replied that my excitement level was a five.

"Okay. Can you share with me why you're a five, yet you've partially put your heart and soul into the opportunity?"

Sure, that was easy.

"I just don't see it as a fit for me. I'm not a politician; I'm a community leader who's passionate about connecting people and building healthy communities. I'm not attracted to the polarizing nature of politics and the lies and mistruths that politicians throw around. It seems really ugly and unhealthy.

So, my attitude is: 'if I'm supposed to serve in this capacity, I will. And if I'm not, I won't.'"

What I'd said made total sense to me—put myself halfway out there and see what transpired.

I felt Heather's amusement through the phone. She had a way of pausing for a moment and being very intentional with her words when she was about to share something profound.

"So, here's the thing. We have a vision for our work and plot the path we feel makes sense for us to move forward in this work. You're making an impact on the health of our community, no doubt about it. But perhaps the Universe is trying to offer you another way to impact this community's health through a new lens that you had never before considered? Are you shying away from the gift presented to you, which could be way more impactful than your current path?"

Her response had some truth to it. How many times had I thought I knew the best way to accomplish something, only to find myself off track and on a new path? This Commissioner role would provide a platform to create policies for a sustainable, connected community. I'd be able to share the importance of how we build our community, from infrastructure to density, and support diverse populations of people, bringing us together to reduce stress and tension. As I reflected on her words, I realized this could be very impactful work.

"I hear you, Heather. You make a great point. I hadn't thought of it that way, but now that you mention it, it makes perfect sense."

Then, there was the second pause. Again, sensing the smile creeping onto her face as her pupil began to understand the lesson, my intuition told me there was more to come. As usual, my intuition didn't disappoint me.

"So, now that you're truly open and ready for a new possible way for you to promote the health and healing of southwest Florida, how are you going to approach it? I get the thought process behind, 'If it's meant to be, it'll be.' But while that may be true, it doesn't mean that you should only halfway go for it. If you're willing to move forward and open yourself up to this potential opportunity, you have to go for it 100 percent. You have to laser focus on it and give it all you've got while remaining unattached to the outcome."

As my mind tried to process this new information, my heart was beating out of my chest. Wow. That wasn't how I approached things at all. When it came to putting myself out there, in order to be safe, I maintained a laissez-faire attitude and would not attach to the outcome. I'd always put half of my heart and soul into things. When it came to things outside of myself, I have 110 percent. Work, check. Family, check. Friendships, of course. But when it came to me, I was unable to open myself up to that much vulnerability. With my approach, if and when something didn't work out, I wasn't fully invested, so I could weather the disappointment. Isn't that how life was supposed to work?

Heather's suggested method was completely new to me. And it landed; I needed to be laser focused and give it all I've got, unattached to the outcome.

Heather and I spent the next two hours on the phone, incessantly chatting away and squeezing in as much heartfelt knowledge as we could convey. The car ride flew by, and before I knew it, I had arrived in Coral Gables and was on-track to be late for my first gathering. We said our goodbyes, and I profusely thanked her for her friendship, inspirational leadership, and never-ending support.

As I walked into the Biltmore Hotel, it was as if I was walking on air. I had a newfound way of seeing things. I was going to put myself out there fully and authentically while being unattached to the outcome. I felt like I was ten years younger and twenty pounds lighter. What a concept to live by!

My energy was through the roof as I reconnected with my amazing classmates. They felt it too. One by one, calmly and with youthful excitement, I shared with them that I had just applied as a candidate for the Governor's appointment of the recently vacated County Commission seat in Lee County. The authentic offerings of congratulations and support were breathtaking. Our class leader made an announcement about my new endeavor as we started our meeting, and everyone brought out their phones, reaching out to their contacts in Tallahassee to share their support.

I found myself blushing as I sat in uncharted territory. I had officially put myself 100 percent out there with zero guarantees of the outcome. And within minutes, fifty-four of the most vibrant, impactful leaders from around the state were working their phones, putting their support behind me on both sides of the aisle. All genders. All races. They had spent a year getting to know me, and they believed in me. Without any hesitation, they offered their wholehearted support. I felt so alive, so seen, so understood, and so unattached to the outcome.

MY STINT
AS A POLITICIAN

JULY 2019

In mid-July, I received an exciting call from the Governor's Chief of Staff saying I would be the new Commissioner. I was so grateful that my hard work and dedication had paid off. Before the final press release could go out, he would need to make three calls to big donors, as it was only right to let them know before hearing the news publicly. I waited for the call back.

The Chief of Staff didn't sound as peppy as he did during our first conversation. He questioned how "Republican" I was, noting my past with Planned Parenthood and a one-time donation to a Democrat. He assured me to sit tight, and that he'd get back to me, which gave me reassurance that I'd passed the test. I'd done it; I was going to be a Commissioner and could make a difference in a new exciting role!

Twenty-one days after the Chief of Staff's call, word got out that the Governor was going to be making a very important announcement at a press conference in the county north of us at noon. *Hmm. I wonder what's going on. Did I miss my call? Oh well, I can't wait. I bet they just want to get my reaction on camera. I'd better get ready, as the TV crews are sure to arrive shortly.*

Precisely at 11:45 a.m., my phone rang. It was a Tallahassee number. It was a junior person on the Governor's Staff.

"Mrs. Collins, I'm calling from the Governor's office. Thank you for your application for Lee County Board of County Commission. The Governor has decided to go in a different direction, and we wanted to thank you for your interest in this appointment."

Wow.

Fifteen minutes later, it was all over the news that the Governor had appointed yet another white male to the Lee County Board of County Commission. Ironically, he chose someone who never even applied.

Later, I learned I was the only applicant who had received the "sorry you didn't get the job" call.

As I sat in my home office and absorbed all of these blows, I texted my husband and a few close friends who had been walking this opportunity closely with me. My phone began to blow up, and I watched it shake on my desk. They were angry that the whole story wasn't told. I had chosen to sit quietly with my end of the story, as to not disrupt the outcome. I sat in front of my computer screen and started typing an email to my husband. I had to output my experience and my feelings in real time. This would go nowhere but to David and would merely be an exercise to help me heal and release.

As I typed, I envisioned the community leaders who wrote letters to the Governor on my behalf—those who had aligned their reputation with mine and would never know the whole truth. I felt horrible that twisted truths might come out and that these potential lies might hurt their reputation. I was devastated that their support of me might hurt their community standing or businesses. It took less than twenty minutes to type my experience and send the email to my husband that Friday afternoon. After hitting send, I released a long, exhausted exhale. I let myself feel hurt, yet I congratulated myself for the way I managed my journey: quietly, honestly, and divinely.

I came to and worked to regroup. How many more hours would it be before David would be home from work and we could privately digest this crazy experience? I revisited my computer screen and saw an email from David. *That's strange. We almost never connected while he was at work, and he most certainly never checks his personal email during the workday.* I soon realized he must have opened the email I just sent him. What a sweetie.

I opened his reply and was taken aback by his response. It only contained four letters in total.

"SEND"

"SEND?" *What does he mean? Send this email out? Really?*

My intent was to simply get things off my chest and share them with David, not to share them with the outside world. Would he really be ok with me sending this?

Wow. I'd love to share this. I could tell the truth before it got twisted all around. Then, those who aligned with me would know proactively. But would David really be ok with that?

I replied to his email, asking, "Really? Are you okay if I send this to the few dozen folks who wrote letters on my behalf?"

Within a few hours of the noon press conference, I sent this email to my closest supporters who had put themselves on the line in support of me.

The email read,

> Friends, it is with deep and humble gratitude that I thank you for your encouragement & support for the appointment to the Lee County Board of County Commission. It moves me beyond words, as you selflessly walked beside me on this journey. Because of this, I want to take a moment to share with you a summary of this experience as I contemplate, learn, and grow from it.
>
> On July 11th at 12:02 p.m., I received one of several calls from the Governor's Chief of Staff, excited to share that the Governor had selected me for the vacant District 3 County Commission seat. He stated

that he is now working on the press release and would be sending it out within two hours. Before he'd hit send, he had to make three calls: two to big local Republican donors and one to the acting chair of the Board of County Commission. They felt it best these folks heard the news directly from the Governor's Office before it hit the press. He said he would call me back within two hours and would send the release. I thanked him and told him I'd wait to hear back from him.

A few hours later, he did call me back and immediately asked if I had hosted fundraisers for democratic candidates. I replied that I hadn't hosted any fundraisers for democratic candidates. I did share that in 2018, I attended a local gathering to meet Nikki Fried who was running for Commissioner of Agriculture. A wonderful Republican friend who felt Ms. Fried would make an excellent Commissioner extended me the invitation. Ms. Fried is a Democrat. After hearing her message celebrating pro-business, pro-growth, pro-agriculture, and pro-hemp, my husband and I gladly donated to her campaign.

The second question he asked me was whether or not I was affiliated with the REC (Republican Executive Committee). I replied that I wasn't a part of the REC.

The third and final question was in reference to my stance on women's reproductive rights. He brought up the fact that I support Planned Parenthood. I calmly began to explain that the County Commission doesn't make decisions regarding this issue, but I still expressed that I don't sit in judgement of women who choose to have abortions. Many decades ago, I was robbed of the opportunity to have children, and I choose not to judge others.

In June 1990, a month after graduating from college, I was unemployed and uninsured. I found myself meeting a young man and realizing I might get involved with him. I sought birth control, and, thankfully, a friend told me about a free health clinic a few miles away in New Haven.

After they examined me at the clinic, they didn't give me birth control. Instead, they asked me to come back the following week so a physician from Yale who donates one lunch hour of his week to the clinic could examine me. I wasn't pleased, but, by the grace of God, I went back the following week. Within twenty-four hours, I found myself on an operating table at Yale-New Haven hospital having exploratory surgery. I woke up eleven hours later to learn that I had ovarian cancer and that the surgeon had removed both of my ovaries. I was twenty-one years old with zero symptoms and zero health insurance, and this accidental discovery literally saved my life. So yes, I have shared many times that Planned Parenthood saved my life.

Unfortunately, I didn't get to share this entire story, as he stopped me a few sentences in by saying, "I know, I read the article." I still to this day don't know to which article he was referring, since most interviews I've done include this story. I always come back to it when an interviewer asks me, "Why are you so positive?" or "What experience most impacted your life?" Finding this cancer so fatefully at a free health care clinic in the middle of New Haven showed me that I was left on this earth for some reason bigger than me. And still, to this day, I take that responsibility very seriously.

As our conversation came to a close, the Governor's Chief of Staff told me to sit tight and that he'd be back in touch. He also said that when he sends out the press release, I should use this office when connecting with the media. I shared that I would be happy to do that and appreciated the opportunity.

I never heard from him again.

For the past twenty-one days, I've sat with this experience. I chose to remain quiet so that the process would work itself out without my interference. Today, as we learn who will fill this seat, I choose to reach out to you and share my story because of your gracious support. I'm at peace knowing that this experience has made me a stronger, more whole person. I proudly stand by my morals, values, honesty, and integrity. I embrace my collaborative mind and the fact that I don't follow the crowd just because I'm a part of it. I take each and every person and issue individually and make the best decision

I can. Nikki Fried has *no* idea who I am or that my support of her has forever changed the trajectory of my life. Yet, I will forever be thankful that I chose to support her. After years and years of donating only to Republican candidates, this one-time, fateful donation has been an incredible gift showcasing my core belief in convening and co-existing.

I applaud amazing women who are tirelessly shedding light on the vital importance of access to health care and family planning. Barbara Pierce Bush, whose Republican daddy and grandaddy ran our country, visited Naples this winter sharing this exact message at a Planned Parenthood fundraiser: https://www.gulfshorelife.com/2018/01/30/barbara-bush-and-the-battle-for-womens-health/. US Senator Susan Collins (R-ME) also received their 2017 Barry Goldwater Award which recognizes Republican lawmakers who champion reproductive health care issues and who work to ensure rights granted to women.

I am a Republican woman who can see the good in the other side, who supports access to health care and family planning, and who has spent two decades in this community working toward a healthier, happier, more connected community. My story isn't one about membership in one particular political party; it's also not about Planned Parenthood. Shame on those who made it about that.

This week, in my daily mediation practice, Deepak Chopra shared, "Use your energy to heal and transform." And this I will. This polarization needs to stop. This hate and fear need to stop. This judgement needs to stop. We're hurting ourselves and one another. We're destroying our planet. We're toxifying our water supply, our air, and our minds. I'm forever thankful for this experience and for the twenty-one-day reflection. I know deep in my soul that the answers are available if we choose to sit quietly long enough to hear them.

From the bottom of my heart, thank you. I'm forever in gratitude for your love and support,

Christin.

The journey was never about being County Commissioner. It was about being appointed, then not being appointed, based on truths that I was proud of—truths that made me uniquely me. I didn't blindly follow the crowd, but instead expressed my individual thoughts and beliefs. To this day, people apologize to me for how the Governor's office treated me. It makes me smile. There was absolutely nothing to be sorry about. This was an incredible experience—one for which I'm forever grateful. It helped me dig deep, learn who I was, and stand quietly and comfortably in that truth.

LOBBY BAR

———

AUGUST 2019

Early in 2019, Scott Kashman and I received an email from WELCOA (the Wellness Council of America) asking if we would like to co-present at their national conference in August in Philadelphia. Words couldn't express my excitement. How incredible that they selected my former boss and I to share our journey of health and healing with the summit attendees!

This was a doubly exciting opportunity, as Scott and I no longer worked together at the hospital. Earlier in the year he'd taken on a new role, which meant that I reported to someone else. I was miserable. Under this different system leadership, the health and wellness movement no longer received the support it once had. Every day was a battle, and my job took the wind out of my sails. The thought of reconnecting with Scott on this project and presenting nationally on our work together reignited a spark that had all but faded away.

Scott called me immediately, asking if I had read the email.

"What do you think?"

What do I think? I think it's awesome!

I'd get to fly to Philly, co-present with my favorite colleague, and inspire all kinds of folks to further their well-being journey. Plus, we'd get to spend the next eight months preparing the presentation together, taking us into deep reflection and exploration of the work we had done thus far.

"Are you kidding? I'm in! What do *you* think?"

"Okay, let's do it."

So once again, the universe had provided a way for me and Scott to continue our journey together, against the odds and under the radar.

To be transparent, Scott did most of the leg work. He was so talented at translating the crazy, innovative, disruptive ideas that we co-created. He made them accessible to folks by systemizing them and making them tangible for corporations to digest and implement. After reviewing our content, the title of our presentation revealed itself as "Interconnected: Creating Sustainable Change Through Inspired Leadership." This title truly captured the foundation of our work together over the past half decade, and so did our presentation. Our goal was to showcase humble servant leadership, deeply connecting as a team, and weaving together the diverse ideas and thoughts of a team to create meaningful, sustainable change. With this as the foundation, we could create a healthy work environment that supported the growth and evolution of each team member, making them more vibrant at work as well as at home and in their communities at large.

As we made arrangements to participate in this conference, we decided that Scott would fly in the day before our presentation and fly out the following day immediately after we finished. I, too, would fly up the day before, but would remain at the conference to attend the speaker dinner that WELCOA was hosting as a wrap-up. There would be some incredible presenters taking the stage and we felt it would be beneficial for me to connect with them during the intimate gathering. I was excited to attend and looked forward to the adventure.

It was always magical to get off-campus with a colleague outside of the constraints of work. We landed in Philadelphia just in time to check into the hotel and head out to dinner. I began to relax and enjoy the ease of being on the road, as new experiences and travel truly light me up. We had dinner plans at one of my favorite vegan restaurants in the United States, Vedge. I'd been there a few times and was excited to share it with Scott. Vedge does an incredible job creating delicious vegan food in a swanky, upscale environment. Scott went to undergrad in Pennsylvania, so one of his college roommates would be joining us for dinner. Getting to see my former boss with his college friend, swapping stories about the past and hearing about the good ole days also added a special twist.

After dinner, I parted ways with the boys so they could catch up more deeply. I enjoyed an evening city walk back to the hotel. As I snuggled into bed that night, I felt whole and grateful.

The next day, after an extensive brisk walk around the city and an hour of SoulCycle, I cleaned up my act and was growing even more excited to co-present with Mr. Kashman. Nothing felt better than knowing someone has your back, brings out the best in you, and has unique talents that coincide with yours.

We welcomed guests as they arrived, and I felt the energy in the room intensify. We spent the next hour flowing through our presentation. I cherished co-presenting with Scott. It was as natural as breathing and as satisfying as it gets. Scott talked about some technical aspects of interconnected leadership, and I shed light on servant leadership and casting a vision of love. I enjoyed the adrenaline running through me as I made eye contact with many of the guests and witnessed their heads nodding in agreement with many of the points I discussed.

We landed our presentation, expressed gratitude for the opportunity to connect, and bid farewell to our guests. As often happened, attendees lined up to share a highlight or a relevant life experience, as well as to ask a deeper question. I always loved this part. Scott attracted folks who would bring up their pens and notepads and ask operational questions. My line would fill up with people who were incredibly introspective, asking soulful questions that lit me up. We spent another thirty or so minutes individually chatting with the final guests. With the room finally empty, we high-fived each other, celebrating another amazing, shared experience.

To say I was on cloud nine was an understatement. Work those days was filled with mixed emotions and experiences.

Unfortunately, more days were frustrating rather than fulfilling. We'd seen changes in leadership at our hospital, and our new leaders didn't embrace our work like the previous ones had. Days like this fueled me with the hope and inspiration I needed to keep going.

I thanked Scott as he hustled off to catch his flight home. I stepped out onto the city streets and I headed to one of my favorite hotel lobby bars in the United States. It was time to celebrate and reflect on a job well done.

I had been to the Philadelphia Ritz Carlton lobby bar a number of times. It stood out as an elegant, spacious, hip atmosphere with amazing craft cocktails. I cherished bellying up to the swanky bar and enjoyed soaking it all in. This was the absolute perfect place to venture to after a successful presentation. I sat quietly and celebrated as the joy of the moment permeated. The bartender surprised me with a vodka-based treat of his selection and presented a delicious bowl of sweet and salty treats to nibble on. I took out my phone, and noticed a text from Scott. His 4:00 p.m. flight had been delayed until 8:00 p.m.

"Where are you? I'll pop by and we can celebrate our presentation."

"I'm at my favorite lobby bar."

Ironically, that was all I had to say. He had heard me talk about this spot so many times, he knew exactly where to find me.

About twenty minutes later, Scott sauntered in. Whenever I saw him, a smirk would erupt on my face. His comedic personality permeated any room the minute he entered it, even one as big as this lobby bar. I waved to get his attention, thoroughly happy to be sharing the next hour toasting our success.

Scott ordered a matching vodka drink, and we spent a few minutes discussing the excitement of our presentation. We both agreed that we had touched lives and helped to support the wellbeing of the attendees and their perspective companies. He teased me about the crowd that gathered after we finished, and how excited I became when I presented and connected. To his defense, he hadn't seen me excited in quite a while. It felt good to be creating and inspiring awakenings again. As we reflected, I heard Scott softly ask me a question.

"What are you doing?"

His question didn't compute.

"What do you mean what am I doing?"

"I mean, what are you doing at home. With work. You're so disengaged. It's hard to watch you like this."

Immediately I felt intense heat sweep over my body.

Are you kidding me? I'm trying my hardest to plug in, but leadership continually disregards me and puts me out to pasture.

"I can't believe you of all people are saying this to me! You know what I'm up against. You know that I'm trying to make an impact and that my words are falling on deaf ears. So, what am I doing? I'm waiting for you to go find a new job in a culture that embraces wellness. Then I'm going to come work for you."

Scott was a smart man. He smiled and let it go.

As history had proven, this girl could hold a grudge. My lobby bar drink, and quite frankly my entire night, had now been officially ruined.

Is he for real? What does he expect me to do?

I did my best to let it go, but I couldn't slow down my heart rate. I was definitely crushed.

We somewhat successfully small talked for a bit longer and grabbed a bite to eat at V Street. Then it was time for him to pick up his luggage back at the hotel and head to the airport. Instead of walking back with him, I decided to remain at V Street by myself. I had nowhere to be and, quite frankly, didn't want to continue talking as if nothing was wrong any longer. I bid him farewell and watched him turn and walk out the door.

As his silhouette disappeared out of the restaurant, my heart sank. I wanted to say, *"Wait, come back!"* or *"Wait, I'll walk back with you!"* I could be pigheaded sometimes. Stubbornly sitting there, upset and off-kilter, I ordered another drink and felt sorry for myself.

My head was spinning.

How dare he. He knows what I'm up against. He knows I'm trying my hardest. He knows I just want things to go back to how they were when we were able to vision cast and co-create as the national leaders that we are.

Basically, I sat at V Street for the next hour sulking into my beverage, incredibly pissed off.

Then it was closing time. I willed myself off my bar stool and slowly sauntered back to the hotel. The lights in the City of Brotherly Love exuded an ironic backdrop, as I felt conflicted and sad.

I miss what I had. I know what I want, but I have no idea how to get there.

One of the very, very few people who truly got it and whom I truly trusted, just crushed me. City lights usually fired me up. That night, I found them lonely and empty.

Back at the hotel, I climbed into bed and cried. I felt my heartbreak and sadness overtake me. I kept replaying his words in my mind, and my anger escalated.

It's not my fault. I've tried.

What else was I supposed to do besides try to weather this horrible storm? Out of nowhere, a new thought entered my mind.

That must have been really hard for him to say to me.

The more I thought about it, the more I realized that it actually took courage and true friendship for him to address this with me. If he didn't care, he wouldn't have wasted his $30 vodka and dampen the mood. He would've kept things topical, and we would've toasted our success and moved on.

But, today he saw the real Christin again. The Christin he met at Bennett's seven years earlier. The vibrant, carefree, fun loving, bubbly human whose joy and positivity were infectious. He hadn't seen this me in quite a while. Present-day Christin was pissed off, bitchy, complaining, judgmental, and downright energy sucking. So, maybe he was just trying to point out to me that I'd been giving away my power and joy. Maybe today during our presentation he saw that spark again.

Wow. I'm a bitch. This poor guy was just trying to help me, and I wasn't open to his constructive feedback. I suck.

I fumbled for my phone and called him. Thankfully, his flight hadn't taken off yet. He was on the plane waiting for pushback.

"Hi. It's me."

Before he could reply, I continued,

"I've been thinking about what you said to me tonight at the lobby bar. I didn't like what you had to say. This has been a very, very difficult professional chapter for me. I'm realizing that it was probably hard for you to bring this up to me.

It actually took real friendship to have this conversation, especially because you probably knew it wouldn't go over well."

Without taking a breath, I continued slowly and with humility.

"I owe you an apology. I'm sorry I didn't see it as a gesture of true concern. I do now. I'm mortified that I've sold myself so short, waiting for others to save or direct me. I've given away my power and my joy and act like a wounded animal. I appreciate you calling me out, and I'm sorry that I was such a bitch."

I could feel Scott smiling over the phone.

"I knew it wouldn't go well, but you are indeed correct. Today, you were so illuminated. You were on point, creating and inspiring like you do so well. It makes me sad to watch you dying a slow death at work. I was just trying to gently help you see the truth."

I was at a loss for words. I let the silence speak for itself.

"I have to go. We're about to push back. I'm glad that you figured this out, and I'm glad you did before I had to sit through this three-hour flight knowing how mad you were at me!"

After we hung up, I lay in bed, mortified and embarrassed.

When did I get so needy? When did I give up my power, my journey, and my badass self?

How humiliating. I'd been sitting around sulking, waiting for someone else to fix my problems. Needless to say, I didn't sleep restfully that night. I tossed and turned all night, fitfully moving from embarrassment to heartfelt gratitude and back again. How blessed was I to have such a true friend, and how ridiculous of me to think that he—or anyone else—could save me?

134 BITS OF
INFORMATION

———

DECEMBER 2019

David and I had been trying to get together with Heather Christie and her husband, but once again, our schedules didn't seem to line up. Too much time was passing by and too many obstacles stood in the way. Eventually, Heather and I decided not to wait on our husband's shared availability. Instead, we planned a rare girls-only get together at a swanky new bar in Naples.

As I drove the hour south to meet Heather, I reflected on the many revelations with which her friendship had blessed me. Years earlier, while she served as the president of the east coast chapter of the Florida Speakers Association, she invited me to attend a meeting as her guest. From this experience, I learned to buy my own domain name. Then I created my YouTube page. I also learned that there was an actual science behind the art of public speaking. Heather began to provide concrete feedback for me after I gave a public talk. She would help me critically think through how to grow profession-ally. Finally, there was that key moment I learned to "go for it, unattached to the outcome." Little did I know, tonight was going to provide yet another of those infamous turning points in my mindset.

I was very attracted to Naples' vibe and was excited to meet with Heather at the bar she had chosen. It was a plush, well-manicured, hip place to be that combined some of the cultural elements of city life with the class of affluence and the ease of the tropics. It definitely spoke to my soul. It was good to be back, and doubly as good to be spending the eve-ning enjoying fine wine, food, and conversation.

Heather and I nestled into a relatively quiet corner so we could catch up. Our table had a great view of the other guests so we could admire and wonder about them. As usual, our conversation was rapid and energetic. There was always such an explosive exchange between us as we rushed to get it all in during our visits. We weaved in and out of topics such as work, politics, health, public speaking, spirituality, and marriage. We had so much in common.

As we landed on the subject of marriage, I shared an upsetting disagreement David and I had recently. Of course, as hus-band and wife in a twenty-year relationship, we were going to have fights from time to time. But this one I couldn't quite release. I wanted desperately to solve it and prevent this from happening in the future as much as possible. I hated fighting. I was terrible at it. I used to be a professional runaway-er. I had no concept of how to fight. Growing up, my parents had never fought—in front of me and my brother, anyway.

My first husband and I never spoke a harsh word to one another. I'll never forget when I was in therapy trying to work through my divorce. The first question my therapist asked me was,

"How do you and your husband fight?"

What a silly question.

I proudly replied, "We never fight."

So, why are we getting a divorce? Why did things not work out? We got along great!

Then, I heard my therapist's response.

"Well, there's the first problem. Everyone fights at one point or another. No two people on this earth have exactly the same wants, needs, and desires. So, one of you wasn't being true to yourself when differences arouse. All relationships have moments of disagreement. The key is how you work through them."

Wow. Doesn't that make sense. No two people are alike, so occasionally, differences should reveal themselves.

That night with Heather, I shared how worried I was that David and I had this argument, yet how thankful I felt to be able to sit through the discomfort of it and remain centered and calm. The old me would've packed a bag and ran as far away as possible to avoid the pain of conflict.

I watched that knowing smile of hers grow as she leaned forward with excitement. Her eyes glittered with the wisdom that she was about to share.

"For every second during any given time, there are roughly two million bits of information that are coming at us. Two million! And our brain has the capacity to absorb—get ready—134 bits of information per second. That's all!"

Without doing the math, I let that sink in. How complex it was in our modern-day society that bombarded us with information to process things.

She continued.

"How we manage this is by identifying patterns and make assumptions as quickly as possible, immediately discarding any information that we think we recognize as familiar. We file that away as information we already know and understand."

I nodded my head in understanding.

"This truth, of course, is based on our past biases and experiences. So, we grab this seemingly familiar chunk and file it in one part of our brain. Then, we mitigate the next chunk and move it away to another part. We drill down to 134 as quickly as possible so we can process this 'truth' and continue on our merry way."

She paused and let that information sink in. As I processed what she'd said, I realized it made excellent sense. We simple humans could only process 134 pieces of information per second, yet the engineering of today's culture offers up over two million, so thank goodness we could default the majority of it based on our past experiences.

As was probably her intention, I realized that if I looked at a situation through the lens of my life's experiences and biases, there were zero other people on the planet who had the same lens—not my brother, not my best friend, and not my spouse. No one.

"Heather, that's incredible. It's literally impossible for anyone else to see something the same exact way I do. There will always be at least a slight variation of the truth for them based on their own experiences and life history."

"Yes!" Heather exclaimed as I grasped the concept.

More lightbulbs turned on for me.

"This is exciting yet confusing at the same time." I paused. "So, everyone has their own truth. Everyone sees things a little differently, but they're correct, too! How do we possibly function as a society? Since everyone has their own truth, how did we ever come together to live in relative peace and harmony?"

While we didn't manage to solve that last question, I did leave our get-together with another amazing mind shift from my transformative friend, Heather Christie. We all see things differently, and there's a very valid reason why we do: we all have different truths based on our different experiences.

I found myself looking at many different situations I'd experienced, now understanding that I had been judging them based on my own defaults and biases. I took a pause and contemplated what other 1,999,866 bits of information existed that I'd already swiped away. What truth was my husband seeing? What truth was my boss seeing? What truth was that stranger seeing? Sometimes we know, and sometimes we have to be comfortable with the fact that we'll never know.

I now try to open myself up to contemplate other ways to view any given moment in time. In doing so, I let go of things I can't control and try not to judge others who are on their own path. This way of thinking has reduced my stress and allowed me to appreciate the diverse thinking of others. That night at the bar in Naples proved to be yet another step toward optimal wellbeing and another lesson from my friend Heather Christie.

THE DAY I KNEW I HAD TO LEAVE HEALTH CARE

———

JANUARY 2020

Each quarter, a few hundred leaders from the health care system come together to receive an update from senior leadership on pertinent information, strategic direction, and celebration. We would spend a few hours in our local performing arts hall, gathered to connect with one another and align our focus.

I attended many leadership meetings where there was deep, detailed discussion about the current state of health care. The United States spends more on health care than any other country, yet our health care outcomes are consistently among the worst in the world. The model has long been broken and is only getting worse, so leaders have been scrambling to try to navigate escalating revenue reduction paired with worsening of health care outcomes. Obesity continues to rise. Mental health continues to decline. Every day at work was doom and gloom.

As I sat in these meetings, I was haunted by the same baseline questions: "Why are we waiting for people to get sick before we help them? Why aren't we working to discover the root cause of illness? Why aren't we connecting the dots across all of people's different ailments and looking at their environment to help aid resolve?" As the System Director of Health and Wellness, I was trying to raise awareness about these baseline questions and trying to shift to promote prevention and a holistic approach to wellbeing. Unfortunately, my efforts and questions fell on deaf ears. The system was simply not designed that way. So, I continued to die a slow death in my role, knowing that I wasn't the pioneer who would completely shift how our nation approached health care.

That particular day during the quarterly leadership meeting, we would be hearing from a consultant out of Washington, DC, who was going to update us on the state of affairs of health care in the United States. I was excited to hear what he had to say, as he was definitely the expert. We had invested top dollar to learn from him. I looked around the room and contemplated the pay of those sitting in this auditorium. Hundreds of our top leaders sat, ready to listen. I couldn't imagine how much this meeting was costing, between salaries and consulting fees, but I was hopeful that it would lay a foundation that we could use to springboard into a new direction and stop spending so much on health care and getting the worst outcomes.

The consultant took the stage and launched into his presentation. He had great stage presence, commanding energy, and an impressive slide show. He walked us through the decline in reimbursement, insured patients, and health outcomes—all of the statistics that depressed me daily. I digested this information and remained excited as I waited for him to pivot and show us how we were going to overcome our situation to create a new, vibrant future.

Thirty minutes went by, but the pivot never came. He offered neither a solution nor an innovative way to approach health. He simply shared the same bad news, but from a different source: we needed to cost save as much as possible. The future looked bleak. Things weren't working.

My heart broke. He, after all, was the rock star expert from out of town who we had flown in to inspire us and help us navigate through this broken chapter. Yet, he offered absolutely nothing new or helpful. What I *did* hear was the backs of our staff breaking, as we would have to attempt to squeeze more out of them instead of focusing on their wellbeing. Why are patient experience scores not going up? Probably because we tax our staff to the point of sheer exhaustion. The system was broken, and it didn't seem like we were going to fix it.

As the consultant thanked us for our attention and exited the stage, I exhaled. Normally, this type of information made my blood boil and my heart race.

I would usually want to stand up and scream, *"Doesn't anyone else see this? We're doing it wrong! We're treating the symptoms and not getting to the root cause of the problems. This is insane! We only invest* after *people get sick, instead of helping them* not *get sick. Why can't we talk about how to help people be well and thrive?"*

But on that day, my reaction was different. It was surreal, almost like an out of body experience. I was done being frustrated. I was finished trying to convince others to see what I saw. I was done trying to make the *Titanic* float by duct taping the holes and hoping for the best. The system was broken. I couldn't fix it. All I could do was know my truth.

As I left the meeting and walked to my car, I called David.

"Hey, babe! How's your day going?" he asked.

"Hi, honey. I'm just leaving this morning's leadership meeting where we heard a presentation from a national expert on health care. Unfortunately, there was nothing innovative or uplifting that came out of it. We still have no clarity on how to correct the course."

He concurred that health care was incredibly complex and that disruption might have to come from outside of health care.

It felt surreal to share my takeaway:

"If this consultant didn't have the answers, I doubt anyone within health care will. My spirit is free, I'm no longer frustrated. It's not their fault. The system isn't broken; it's working perfectly, as it was designed."

Our current health care system was designed to treat people after they get sick by reacting to or repairing their symptoms. It didn't look at the whole person for a root cause. It trained clinicians to engage with patients for only minutes at a time and to medicate or operate on these symptoms. Providers were paid to repair instead of prevent. People in the United States were getting sicker and sicker. Obesity was at a record high, as was chronic disease. Eighty-five percent of chronic disease is preventable or reversible, yet we still address patients after the fact without solving for the core problems. Yes, the system was working perfectly as designed.

When I reflect upon moments in history, I see that true disruption rarely happens within an industry; even Kodak declined the idea of digital photography. It's hard to see the forest from among the trees. And our society rarely celebrates innovators who are pre-pioneering new ways to look at things. Often, people think they're crazy and outcast them as misfits.

The time had come for me to untether myself from health care and follow my calling. I needed to speak up and share my own health journey, to divulge my root cause and trauma healing, to open up about the unique experiences that I've had, and how I discovered that the mind-body connection is foundational to living a vibrant life of optimal wellbeing.

PART 5

RISING TO NEW BEGINNINGS

EPILOGUE

———

NOW.

2020: the year of a global pandemic that has brought complete disruption, untethering, surprises, and opportunities to look at things in new ways—sometimes not by choice.

This crisis ushered in incredible new opportunities to shed light on wellbeing and the vital importance of organizational health. Supporting staff, family, and community during such an unprecedented time brought new ways to showcase resilience, letting go, adapting, and feeling all of our emotions in real time.

Due to the pandemic, the health care system experienced sudden financial hardship, threatening to cause tens of millions of dollars in lost revenue. In an effort to mitigate these losses, my hospital offered a voluntary exit program to staff. While I knew my role within health care was going to sunset over the next few years, I wasn't at a point where I could take this buy out. David and I discussed what I'd do next, as there was no clear path before me.

Twenty-four hours before the mid-June buyout application was due, my husband surprised me by telling me I should take it. He said that we'd would figure it out financially. He knew I was dying inside, and I'm forever grateful that he encouraged and supported me in jumping off the cliff without a parachute and no idea whether or not I could fly.

As life teaches us, it's when we actually make the jump into the unknown that we indeed learn to fly. Opportunities miraculously present themselves, as we soar free, our destination unknown. I've been blessed to spend the past few months reflecting on my journey thus far and writing these insights. At first, they didn't necessarily make sense or seem to tie together. But, as I reread what I've written, I smile at the lessons I learned and those who've helped me learn them. I'm grateful for this great pause which provided me the opportunity to pen these thoughts as part of my healing process. If any of my words can help others to heal, well, that'll be a bonus. By revisiting these moments in my life and fully embracing, feeling, and letting go of each of them, I exhale a deep, grateful sigh.

In October, David and I closed on the sale of our family home. We spent seventeen years there raising our beautiful children, hosting literally hundreds of gatherings, and creating lifelong memories. It was truly a symbolic step toward a new chapter and a reflection on what's actually important and what material things think we need to make us whole.

Our daughter, Meghan, moved out of state and is thriving as a licensed clinical social worker. She spends her days living her passion, helping children face, address, and heal from the traumas in their young lives, or the "Big T's and Little T's" as she calls them. This type of work would be way too devasting for me, yet she's so in her element. She and David talk every morning and we couldn't be more proud of her.

Our son, Brendan, thankfully now lives twenty minutes away from our new condo. He has met the love of his life, and we'll be celebrating their union later this year. We're so thankful for him, their love, and the new family we're melting with. What joy this brings to our hearts.

David continues to support my awakening every day. When we met in late 1999, he saw something in me that I'm yet to fully discover. He is my number one fan, my rock, my supporter, and my biggest cheerleader. Because of him, I've learned to face my issues instead of running from them or ignoring them. I've learned that it shouldn't always be my way and that relationships are two-way streets. We each see things through our own lens, yet we can thrive together in our differences. One of my favorite lessons has been that we can be honest, even when we think the other person isn't going to like what we have to say. That's what true love is.

As for the original team of health care misfits, we are all gone. Dr. Taschner and Dr. Sal have opened a new practice together, Vibrant Beat. Sal stays heavily involved with the American College of Lifestyle Medicine. He practices concierge medicine and is busier than ever helping many, many patients take control of their own health through lifestyle adjustments. Recently, David had his annual checkup with Dr. Sal. When he came home, he shared how refreshing it was to spend so much time with his physician and how he appreciated the deep line of questioning and the holistic approach to his wellbeing.

Scott and Jenny Kashman remain very important friends of ours. He remains one of the nation's premiere health care executives whose leadership will no doubt shift us from reparative medicine to optimal wellbeing.

As for me, I've created my own company to shed light on the vitality of self-love and care. I honestly don't know what the future holds, but for today, I sit, smile, give thanks, take it all in, and marvel at the recent news that my inflammation markers are no longer off the charts!

Thank you for sharing this time with me and reading about my experiences. If it's sparked one intuitive awakening within you, then I've successfully lived my life's purpose.

I'm here to inspire awakening.

My phoenix is rising, and so will yours.

I'm thankful to share this opportunity with you.

be.
love.
CC

ACKNOWLEDGMENTS

—

I'd like to extend a warm thank you to my nieces, Livi and Suni, for their deep-seated inspiration. The day I learned of your conception, I knew I was going to have to tell my story so that you'd be safe and that I wouldn't fail you. It was a reality I knew back in college when my roommate and I would go for long walks and dive deep into conversation. She knew my story and the pain I carried because of it. She wondered why I didn't share it. I also wondered why I didn't share it. There always seemed to be too much at stake; too many lives would be ruined and there would be too much hurt and pain. I could carry it. I *would* carry it. Even then, deep in my soul, I knew if my brother had children someday, I'd have to tell him. I wouldn't be able to live with myself if his kids were traumatized because I kept truth a secret. Livi and Suni, I'm so proud of the young women you're becoming, the way you take on the world, and the way you battle your challenges. You inspire me; you have since before you were born, and I know you always will.

I also feel immense gratitude to my stepdaughter, Meghan Michelle. The day I met you, you were a mighty little spitfire.

Your hair was bigger than your body, your sparkling eyes were full of wonder, and your deep, knowing freckles were like constellations in the galaxy. My heart, which was severely and intentionally tucked away so that it would never be touched or hurt, immediately melted. Since that first fateful night at the hockey game, I knew instantly that I had to be the best woman I could possibly be so that I wouldn't disappoint you. I had to help you grow and be all that you could be. It wasn't a heavy responsibility; it was an ignition. Game on. To see you now, living your purpose and walking your path, makes me so grateful for our shared journey. You're trauma healing. You're elevating consciousness. You're shining bright. Shine on freely and wholly.

My heartfelt thanks goes out to the men in my life—and in this world—who embrace the female spirit. To my husband, David: you're my biggest cheerleader and my sternest coach. To be with a man who isn't threatened by feminine radiance, growth, and expansion has been life changing. Honey, for over two decades, you've challenged me when I wasn't living to my fullest female spirit. Your support and incredible love of your children are the most beautiful things to experience. I've never met anyone like you, and I'm eternally grateful you chose me to experience this life with. To my little brother, Jeffrey: you're one of the most beautiful, kind compassionate souls on the planet. To my stepson, Brendan: your combination of laser focus, determination, and hard work are perfectly balanced with the most loving, open heart. To my former boss and colleague, Scott: you've taught me so much about myself, life, letting go, and what it truly means to live a life of optimal wellbeing. To all of the men who are not threatened by the rise of the feminine: thank you for embracing the balance. Thank you for leading with compassion, nurturing, collaboration, authenticity, and love.

Thank you, cousin Colleen. You've been my soul sister since birth. Sarah Owen, you hold space making all things possible. Much love to Janet Namaste, my healer and guide. To Kurt Maurillo, Joe Bonora, Dawn and Michael Sullivan, Michelle and Peter Vamvakaris, and Debbie and Bill Toler, you believed in me during my darkest hour. Without your investment and support, this phoenix wouldn't have risen.

I express humble gratitude to all who joined in the pre-launch of this book, investing in this story and helping birth it: Donna Caruso, Danielle Fradette, Darla Letourneau, Suzy Clausen, Lisa O'Neil, John Scilipote, Sarah Mitchell, Dena Wiggins, Christine Pottinger, Noelle Casagrande, Jennifer O'Neal, Scott & Dawn Wolf, Scott Tangen, Nicki McTeague, Cindy Brown, Debbie Mikus, James & Cindi Wineinger, Lisa Day, Corinne Wyard, Landen Drake, Bryan Donahue, Darla Bonk, Amy Sanford, Cheryl Schlichte, Barb Stevens, Carolyn Rogers, Anna Toole, Megan Clarke, Cheryl Hill, Eric Koester, Liana Lianov, Kelly Fayer, Cheryl Neal, Joanna Salerno, Michael Agli, Brooke Spencer, Stefanie Edwards, Caprice Woodburn, Cheryl Komnick, Seth Marlowe, Leigh Clark, Susan Blust, Carey Ralston, Frank Wells, Lizbeth Benacquisto, Jennifer Sassi, Andrea Kuzbyt, Natalie Van Horn, Peg Elmore, Lainie Wulkan, Diana Giraldo, Colleen DePasquale, Susan Ryckman, Ellen Cohill, Lora Ulrich, Erika Graziani, Andy Lutkoff, Martha Williams, Judy Williams, Suzanne Boy, Diana Willis, Trish Leonard, Kelly Talamo, Bob Mason, Amy Turner, Samira Beckwith, Lynne Thorp, Mary Gerwig, Jeri Matera, Melissa Mitchell, Sharon Krispinsky, Darcy

Eikenberg, Malena Dorn, Pegine Echevarria, Alison Hussey, and Lauren Drasites. Without your purchase, feedback, words of encouragement, and support, none of this would have been possible.

Thank you Dr. Holly Woods for introducing me to the inspiring Professor Eric Koester. This publishing program was an incredible journey touching lots of lives. To my editors Karina Agbisit and Julie Colvin, your patience, brilliance, and guidance brought out the best in me.

I'd also like to thank those who read this story that I'll never get the chance to meet and those who have a story but don't yet fully own it.

This book was my healing journey that allowed me to pause, reflect, let go, and heal. After almost five decades, I've finally healed. Penning these thoughts was a literal release at a cellular level. Sharing these thoughts is my attempt to plant a seed inside you in hopes of inspiring your awakening.

To all of you: many, many thanks. Together, we will heal and interconnect.

We will rise.

We will be.

We will love.

Made in the USA
Columbia, SC
08 June 2021

39439199R00122